MORE PRAISE FOR
"TOO CRUEL, NOT UNUSUAL ENOUGH"

Life without the possibility of parole is barbaric beyond the definition of the word. As someone who has served a prison sentence, this degree of punishment is unimaginable. Read this collection and gain a glimpse into how the human spirit finds hope in an otherwise hopeless world. Read "Too Cruel, Not Unusual Enough" and then fight for change.

--Wayne Kramer, Artist, Activist, and Co-Founder of Jail Guitar Doors USA

America has long been searching for a humane method of execution. We have gone from hangings, firing squads, electric chairs and gas chambers to the current method of choice, lethal injection. A term of life without parole, in which the person is sentenced to die in prison, is surely America's other death penalty. The voices in this illuminating book of those condemned to death by incarceration show us in no uncertain terms that these men and women suffer a fate that is both cruel and barbaric. There are times when life is harder to bear than death. Life without parole may be one of those times.

--Robert Johnson, Ph.D., Professor of Justice, Law, and Society, American University

I had always felt that justice without mercy is not justice. Thomas Aquinas said *justice without mercy is cruelty,* which is essentially the same thing.

There is a strain in our concept of "justice" which substitutes revenge for justice, where hope is blotted out, where men, often tenuously civilized are, year by year, made incrementally stunted and brutal and lost.

"Too Cruel, Not Unusual Enough" is a collection of writings by some of these men and women, all of whom are serving life sentences in prison without the possibility of parole. The death sentence is cruel; in some ways, LWOP, Life Without Parole, is more cruel. Death, after all, is a cessation of pain. LWOP, these men tell us, is pain without end. Certainly society has a right to exact strong payment for exceptional crime. No civilized society, however, deserves to exact pain without end from its criminals.

Many of the writings in this collection tell of suicide: it is deemed preferable to a life of endless pain. These men have no hope and that perhaps is the cruelest punishment of all.

Nathan Leopold was one of the most notorious killers of the last century: he murdered, for some Nietzschean idea of superman superiority, a fourteen year-old boy. Leopold served 33 years. Upon his release, he spent the next years of his life doing medical work – in prison he had volunteered for malaria testing – dedicating his last years doing good for others. This doesn't have to be an exception, but in our present system it is impossible. These men will never get out; we have banished hope and the idea of redemption and we are wrong in this; this is terrible and unjust. Men must have hope and the possibility of redemption.

"Too Cruel, Not Unusual Enough" reminds us of this in tough, sinewy, powerful words. In Matthew 25:36 it is said: Naked, and ye clothed me; I was sick, and ye visited me: I was in prison, and ye came unto me ... Inasmuch as ye have done it unto one of the least of these my brethren, ye have done it unto me. This book demands of us to live up to our humanity.

--David Scott Milton, novelist, playwright, and screenwriter. His play, "Duet", appeared on Broadway; among his six novels are "Iron City" and "The Fat Lady Sings"; his one-man show, "Murderers Are My Life," is based on his thirteen-year career teaching in maximum-security prisons.

TOO CRUEL,
NOT UNUSUAL ENOUGH

An anthology published by The Other Death Penalty Project

Kenneth E. Hartman, Editor
with John Purugganan and Robert C. Chan, Associate Editors

The Other Death Penalty Project
P.O. Box 1486
Lancaster, CA 93584
www.theotherdeathpenalty.org
todp@live.com

Printed in the United States

ISBN-10: 0615685277
ISBN-13: 978-0615685274

TABLE OF CONTENTS

Too Cruel, Not Unusual Enough

TABLE OF CONTENTS

FUNDER ACKNOWLEDGMENTS

The Other Death Penalty Project

FUNDERS

The Other Death Penalty Project wishes to acknowledge our funders, past and present, without whose generous support we would have been unable to carry out our vitally important work:

Resist, Inc.

United Church of Christ Neighbors in Need Program

A. J. Muste Memorial Institute

The Funding Exchange/Saguaro Fund

Claretians Social Justice Fund

Catholic Campaign for Human Development

The Agape Fund

Very special thanks and immense gratitude to
The Peace Development Fund
whose generous grant made the publication of this book possible.

THE CONTEST

The Other Death Penalty Project

THE CONTEST

In 2010, The Other Death Penalty Project began work on this anthology. We wanted to include all 41,000+ life without parole prisoners throughout the country in its creation, and so launched a writing contest, complete with cash prizes and a nationally-known judge, to encourage people to get involved.

We placed advertisements in *Prison Legal News* and similar publications read by prisoners, inviting submissions of original poetry and prose. We received nearly 300 submissions, all of which were reviewed by The Other Death Penalty Project leadership. Of these, approximately 50 were selected to move on to the next level of judging, to be read by award-winning author and prison reform activist Luis J. Rodriguez.

The winners were selected in August 2011, and the awards published in *Prison Legal News.* Their work is included in this anthology. They are:

1st Place: Dortell Williams, *Making Sense of Life Without the Possibility of Parole*

2nd Place: Robin Ledbetter, *Laying Roots*

3rd Place: Joseph Badagliacca, *Too Cruel, Not Unusual Enough*

The Other Death Penalty Project wishes to thank all the imprisoned writers and poets who participated in our writing contest. We encourage you to keep writing and sending your work out to the free world. With every letter to the editor or op-ed piece that is mailed to a newspaper, or essay or poem submitted to a magazine, society is educated a little bit more that life without parole is truly the death penalty.

PREFACE

Luis J. Rodriguez

Life Without the Possibility of Parole (LWOP) is life without the possibility of life. It's capital punishment on the installment plan. It's without the possibility of redemption, initiation, or restoration.

For forty years, I've spoken out against the death penalty as unjust in a world where those without means - and often with the wrong face, in the wrong time, the wrong place, or with the wrong lawyers - can get put to death while murderers and other criminals with big bucks or different circumstances get to walk out, many not even arrested or, if they do, end up with no convictions.

The naivety of the general culture can't fathom this fact: There are thousands of murderers walking the streets. It's simply not true that the law always gets its "man." The vast majority of these will never murder again. The point is you can't use the ultimate punishment when this depends on factors other than truly blind justice, undeniable evidence, and doing the same thing for everyone - none of which can be guaranteed.

And without a guarantee, anything "ultimate" should never be done.

Besides, the large number of people who have been found innocent since the 1990s proves the fallacy of the whole enterprise. A few states, including my old state of Illinois, have abolished the death penalty in the wake of innocence projects, law university legal clinics, and private lawyers proving there are far too many people on death row that shouldn't be there.

Which to me says nobody should be there.

Now we have Life Without the Possibility of Parole as the alternative. Yet this is also the wrong reaction to the wrongs people commit. It's another ultimate punishment (we're good at words like that, like "shock & awe," that hide more than they reveal). Only recently did I get won over to the understanding that LWOP is another ineffective, meaningless and cruel policy - it should not be used as a substitute for the death penalty. Both are different ways of making sure that a prisoner will only get out of prison feet first.

It goes against one of the main laws of nature, of God if you will, that as long as there is life, a seed, the right environment, a nurturing reality, anything can renew, regenerate, and become better than it was before.

We understand this when it comes to animals, plants, and even in industry. But with human beings, we act as if the laws of nature no longer apply.

The United States has spent some 60 billion dollars a year since the 1980s creating the largest prison systems in the world. Despite this the U.S. has some of the highest number of murders and continues as the largest drug and crime market. The vast expense in tax dollars and broken lives simply has not worked.

The U.S. also stands out among the world's countries, the majority of which do not have LWOP as a sentence. Most of the developed countries don't even have the death penalty. We are behind the times, behind the moral Eight Ball, so to speak. Yet we are also called the "land of the free," one of the most Christian in the world, the supposed bastion of whatever decency still exists on this earth.

Somebody else put that on us, the least we can do is try to live up to it.

It's time our morality, our Christianity if you will, or whatever other spiritualities people practice, and our governmental policies line up - you can't have a belief system that demands one thing of its members and a contrary way of governance. This has created in us a kind of social/cultural schizophrenia that has torn up the relational fabric of this country.

I've been going to prisons and juvenile lockups in the United States for more than thirty years to do talks, poetry readings, as well as writing and other healing workshops. I've gone to maximum-security cellblocks, among lifers, gang members, murderers, and others, and have met some of the most decent, trust-worthy, and capable human beings anywhere. Because of my work, I've been asked to do the same with juvenile and adult offenders in Italy, England, Mexico, El Salvador, Guatemala, Venezuela, Nicaragua, and Argentina, visiting some of the most stark and dangerous institutions of punishment imaginable.

And still I see the seeds of transcendence and possibility wherever I go, even in environments meant to destroy such possibilities.

My own adolescent life involved gangs and heavy drugs, stints in local jails, in juvenile hall, and in two adult facilities, before I changed to a life of writing, community activism, and social justice - only to see my oldest son, Ramiro, end up in the same madness. Ramiro eventually did a total of fifteen years in prison from the age of 17 to 35. Now I've been clean & sober and crime free for almost twenty years. So is my son, who was paroled finally in the summer of 2010. So I've experienced this world of punishment and razor wire as a teacher/writer/healer, and in my personal life.

Still I needed the help of people like Kenneth E. Hartman, a writer/activist presently serving close to 35 years behind bars, and many of the men and women in this anthology, to change my thinking about LWOP. I won't say more - the voices in this book say it all.

- Luis J. Rodriguez, San Fernando, CA, December 24, 2011

MAKING THE
CASE FOR SUICIDE

Michael L. Owens

(Reason #15 anywhere is better than here)

There are of course, the convict favorites: the late night bed sheet torn to strips, braided & looped through the bars after last count, or the old razor blade to the wrists and thighs trick - but those are considered the cowardly outs. I don't know why, quitting is quitting.

The fifth tier is four flights up.
Jumpers are said to have taken "the broken elevator."
You can always tell which are the most committed,
they're the ones who don't scream on the way down.
You're on the fourth tier at a friend's cell arguing the sweetest shot in basketball and then you see this blur of blue, denim and chambray.
Instinctively, you turn from the smacking thump that follows.

Those remembered longest are the kamikazies.
They wait for a guard, with a certain reputation, to look and then run into a crowd with a shank.
They don't stop swinging until the gun tower makes them.

Those soonest forgotten are the overdoses.
They're often ruled unintentional, sometimes they're not.
If it's high quality junk all it takes is a $50 pinch the size of a match head.
Heroin is most popular because they say it's peaceful; one pinprick and you just float away from all the bullshit.

(Reason #8 there's no hope of ever earning redemption)

By the time I was desperate enough to actually consider it as a viable option,
I was already halfway to making my decision.
If I will not be allowed to make amends for my destruction
I should not be expected to sit among the ruins.

(Reason #11 you realize you're becoming someone you hate)

Prison is a cruel trick played on those most deserving of it.

His first two years inside he was so busy trying to learn how to survive he didn't even notice he'd already begun the slow surrender.

After five years he was able to see the sickness in others, the pettiness of it all, the way prisoners die one piece at a time.
He swears he'll never give in to the illness.

Ten years in he begins to experience the strangest fever, and staring out from his reflection, a lonely bitter man holding grudges for a thousand wrongs, real and imagined.

At eleven years eight months and some odd days, he finally understands why every mirror in prison is either scratched or broken.

(Reason #4 the old answers lose meaning)

For the comrade I didn't take seriously,
who made this argument to me and then
went to his cell and hanged himself
We like to take pride in the cliché of having obtained
victory over our sentences and our captors by "transforming"
our cells into a university, a monastery, or even a
healthclub; but that's just how we make ourselves feel
better. Prison isn't a university, it's a breeding ground
for blind conformity to some of humankind's lowest
philosophies. Prison isn't a monastery, it's a nursery for
religious bigotry, hypocrisy, and spiritual con games. We
can't even claim to turn prison into some kind of healthclub.
Cheap, low nutrient foods and sedentary living is killing
us. And those who believe differently are only fooling
themselves.
The sad reality of prison is that most of us exist toward no
positive end. We pass our pathetic days hypnotized by
daytime television. We prey upon our fellow captives of the
state. We drain the resources of free world family, just so
we can buy 200% mark-up pastries and slowly overdose on
trans-fat and cholesterol. All the while the system is more
than happy to go right on using our swollen numbers to
fleece the taxpaying public. So, comrade, it's probably safe
to say that we are well beyond the university, monastery,
healthclub phase of prison culture.

If we were truly committed to our path of resistance,
we would summon the courage to at least deny the system our
passive participation. If we were truly spiritualized
people, we would deny babylon the opportunity to use our
warm bodies for its money schemes. We would flee from this
slave flesh homeward to our God.

(Reason #7 you're tired of having no choices)

wake work eat shower
when and where they tell you to
this can't be my life

life plus seventy
that's what I was sentenced to
I'm just about done

done with watching my
family die, one by one
I am the youngest

(Reason #32 your friends cut ties with you)

Maybe the notion of life w/o is too much
to handle.
Abstract ideas like forever are hard concepts
to comprehend.
How do you measure something that doesn't end,
that just grinds on & on?
How do you explain it to your loved ones?

This is how: you walk up to them, say
I'm dead now
and shoot yourself right then & there.
That has to be close
to what it feels like for family & friends.
Some sentences
can only be explained like that.

My best friend came to visit me
in the county jail, after my sentencing
but before my transfer to san quentin.
He tapped at the window, commenting on
how lax the guards were outside
and how easy it would be for someone
to smuggle in a glass cutter, some cash
and a pistol.
He told me about a history he'd read
and how much he admired the africans who
en route to the americas aboard the slave ships
opted to jump and face the sharks,
preferring death over a life of bondage.

He hasn't come to see me since
and I'm tired of living on coffee and regret.

NOT ALONE

Patrick Angel Acuña

In the twilight of near night the horizon appears to be as uneventful as any tundra. Shadows stretch blackness across the landscape in the surreal orangish illumination of halogen lamps. My attention is fixed on a spot 50 yards beyond my window. There, upon the cooling ground, is what looks to be an outcrop of rock or a clod of dirt.

It is a pigeon with a broken right wing.

For hours I've sat and observed this pigeon desperately flutter and flop, in vain, to take flight. With each failure I can sense fear and exhaustion swiftly building.

Sadly, attempts are becoming less frequent, less spirited, and less hopeful.

Other pigeons gather and circle above their wounded companion. Some have landed and curiously eye the fallen. Concerned, they draw close. Bowing heads they seek to better understand what fate has in store for their feathered-friend. Shortly thereafter, they jump into the sky, circle once, and become dots quickly swallowed by the night.

Forsaken and unmoving, I wonder what set of circumstances brought this particular pigeon to such an unceremonious demise. But was it without ceremony? Could it be that when those others were standing near they were offering a prayer? Or, when circling overhead, a song? Will a mate, sitting on a nest, become confused and wonder of what has become of its partner; will it mourn? Will this soul be missed? Am I not holding vigil for this winged relation? And, why am I doing this?

This prison is built upon a drained lake - a lake the Tule Indian Nation once fished and depended on for subsistence. In a twist of irony, this pigeon landed on the bottom of a lake, fluttered and has been lost. This lakebed, denied water and stripped of vegetation, has become a vast desolation, spotted with fenced-in islands of industrial confinement. This is no place for any of Nature's creation to expire. My spirit grows heavy as I take in the sight before me.

While I consider myself to be sensitive to the plight of all sentient Beings, in truth, what about this lone pigeon has stirred my depths and overwhelmed me with anguish?

I do not want to end like this;
I do not want to die in here;
I do not want to die alone.

I will continue to sit with this unfortunate creature until the last breath; until it flies away and becomes a dot in the spirit-world. I am here to witness, to offer a song, and to whisper a silent prayer. Although condemned to die in prison, just as sure as any death sentence, at least it won't die alone.

LAYING ROOTS

Robin Ledbetter

I wake from my sleep stiff and groggy. When I try to lift my head, it feels heavy, too heavy. My neck is sore. I lie flat on my back on the bed. I feel confused, unsure of where I am and how I got here. I try to swallow, but my throat is burning. As my eyes adjust to the dim light in the room, I stare up at the graffiti-tagged ceiling. Closing my eyes, I shift my head to the right and open them again. I see a heavy door with no doorknob and a large filmy window. The paint on the door is peeling, revealing institutional gray metal; random writing and doodling scar its surface. Outside of the window a man sits, watching me. His face is unfamiliar. Noticing that I am looking at him, he shifts in his seat and lazily picks up a clipboard. He starts writing something.

I turn my head slowly to the left and scan the room. The walls are a faded shade of lilac. There's one small light covered in thick Plexiglas at the base of the wall facing me. In the corner to the left, a metal toilet-sink combination, a window covered in a heavy screen and more Plexiglas. It's dark outside, and I have no idea what time it is. I close my eyes and face the ceiling again.

I recognize this room. I have been here many times before. The paint has changed, and the writing on the wall is different, but it's the same room, the same locked door sealing me into a cell in the mental health unit. As I lay here trying to recall the details of what brought me here again, images replay in my mind.

"Ledbetter, you ready for your shower?" a voice crackles over the intercom in my cell.

"Yes."

Click, the door pops open.

I gather my things, a homemade washrag torn from the end of my towel and the rest of the towel to wash and dry my body, indigent soap and shampoo, and a new pair of red scrubs, the issued uniform in restrictive housing. I also bring a torn, frayed piece of sheet that I ripped from my bedding.

When I get into the shower stall, I place my things on the tub.

"You got fifteen minutes, Ledbetter." Officer Deon says over the intercom. I feel a twinge of guilt because he's a good guy overall, and I don't want to subject him to such a gory scene, but he'll be alright. Things will be better this way. I sit for a few more minutes, reassuring myself that this is the only way for me and everyone else.

"Things will be better this way," I say aloud to myself. I just can't do it anymore.

I don't cry. I just sit until I'm ready. I say a little prayer, and then I tie the sheet around my neck and knot the other end. Standing on the edge of the bathtub, I shut the knotted end in the top of the door, take a deep breath, and jump. The sheet is digging into my neck and squeezing the breath from my lungs. I can feel my feet kicking at the door and my toes sliding back and forth across the tiled floor. My hands are clawing at the wall, hoping for something to ease the weight that's crushing my neck. My face feels like my features are bulging. I hear my name but it seems far away. A low hum rolls through my ears. I'm starting to see spots. I panic and fight for some leverage. I'm suddenly afraid to die.

The next thing I remember is being in the medical unit. There's a swirl of guards and medical staff coming in and out, talking and looking at me. I'm crying, words jumbling out of my mouth. I'm angry that they saved me, yet relieved, but both emotions dissolve into sadness. I'm stripped and fitted into a safety gown of some foreign weighted material.

I sleep.

Tears pour from my eyes as I think of that night. It's not the first time I tried to kill myself and, once again, someone came in the nick of time. I am alive, and I don't really want to be. I have nothing to live for. I'm serving life without the possibility of parole, and that might as well be a death sentence. I will never leave this place, and the thought of that forces any sliver of hope out of me. I have been in jail twelve years.

I came here when I was fourteen years old. I haven't ever lived and now I am supposed to live in jail for at least thirty-eight more years? I'll be sixty-four years old if I get out, and what could I possibly do with my life then? All of my family will be dead. There won't be anything left out there for me. What am I going to do? Get a job? Get an apartment? Finally have some kids? It makes me laugh a bitter laugh to even think of it. I wouldn't even know where to start. I was tossed away by the system when I was just a child and told I was not worth a second chance.

My thoughts turn to a conversation I had with my appellate lawyer.

"Robin, I was reading your PSI and what it said troubles me. I can't believe they viewed your case in that way. How did you feel when you read it?"

"I haven't read it. That's the pre-sentencing investigation right?" I ask. "Why? What does it say?"

"Well, it basically says that with your family history and all the trauma and things you have endured, he recommends a lengthy sentence because you'd be in prison at one point or another. Your family history shows that prison was eventually in your future, so giving you a lengthy sentence will prevent further crimes."

I lie on my back staring at the ceiling, quiet tears trailing down the corners of my eyes and into my hair. I need to change my thoughts. "Na-Na loves John 4-eva" is scrawled on the ceiling, and I try to focus on the pencil markings and empty my mind of all other things, but I can't. I know that I'm more than a career criminal. This was my first time in jail, except for going to juvie for joyriding a little while. I was young, and I messed up. I agreed to steal some money. Rob a taxi driver. I needed the money.

I was homeless and had no family support. I was too young to get a job, and on the streets your options are limited. You basically have three choices: sell drugs, sell yourself, or rob people. Drugs destroyed my family, they ruined my parents; I could never push that poison. I would never sell myself, the fear of rape and HIV canceled that out. Only robbery was left.

No one ever got hurt during a robbery, or so I thought. My father had talked about pulling off robberies whenever I saw him as a kid. Never once did he speak of anything going wrong. He only romanticized it. I can remember, during one of his visits, he drew me a map of a mall he had robbed. There was a smile on his face. I remember the laughter as he recalled falling in his attempts to escape. I remember the far-off look in his eyes when he talked of the bloopers in his criminal acts. He never, not once, warned me or spoke of the risk. And there was risk. It never occurred to me that a robbery could go wrong, except for maybe in the comical ways that my father spoke of. It never occurred to me that someone could die, even after we armed ourselves. It was just to scare the cabbie into giving us the money; that's what we told ourselves and we honestly believed it. The naiveté of two young teenagers.

I remember when I found out our victim had died. I didn't really understand the concept of death. I mean, I did know that when you die, you are buried and gone forever, but I didn't really understand that all life stops. That your family stops. I didn't understand the enormity of the pain of loss to children when parents are snatched away, the devastation of a parent who loses a child. I didn't understand the ripple effect in a community or the tragedy of a life cut short. I didn't appreciate my own life. I had been abused my entire life so I didn't value that life, either. I cared nothing for myself. My self esteem and self worth were shattered. I could not fully understand the value of another human life, as I couldn't understand my own.

In the years I have been in York Correctional, I have learned to appreciate my life. I've learned that I am worthy of love and care and being treated like a person. I learned that I didn't deserve the things I endured growing up, the abuse and neglect from years of childhood trauma. In that process, I've learned the true value of human life and with that knowledge, I came to understand the devastation of my crime. It hit me like a runaway freight train, crushing me and dismantling me. It tore me apart when I realized all of the pain I had caused. I felt like I was drowning in guilt, and that I could never forgive myself for what I did. The beginning of that realization led to my first attempt at killing myself during my incarceration. I didn't want to live with what I did. I spent two weeks in the hospital and came right back to my cell to sit with my guilt, shame, and a need to make amends but knowing that I really couldn't.

Four months after my eighteenth birthday, I was handed down this sentence. I sat in a courtroom and saw the father of my victim look me square in the eye and let me know just how much he hated me. I sat perfectly still, afraid to even breathe as he told the court why I should rot in jail. I didn't feel worthy of breath. I felt as though every molecule in my body was on fire. I felt that I deserved every harsh word he said and deserved to be in jail. I was numb when I heard the judge read the list of charges and the time attached to each. All my feelings and emotions went to my victim's father and to keeping it together in the court. I didn't feel I was allowed the luxury of shedding a tear for myself. It would be disrespectful to the real victims; it would make a mockery of their pain. I thought they'd point an accusatory finger at me and yell, "How dare you act sorry now! How dare you care now? You're looking for sympathy? We're the only ones in pain here, not you! How dare you! How dare you! How dare you!"

"Ledbetter, med-line on the door!" the nurse outside that huge window says. Her voice jars me from my thoughts.

I stare at her for a few seconds, blinking back the memories. Is it worth me moving to get the meds that will quiet my thoughts?

"Do you want them or not?" she says, annoyed. I can see the guard peering at me over her shoulder. He has his clipboard in his hand and when I sit up, he writes on it, marking my progress. I say nothing and take my time peeling the heavy blanket from my body, readjusting the heavy gown. My neck is still really sore, and I shuffle to the door as the trap slams open. I insert my hand through the slot. The nurse places some pills in my hand, and as I put them in my mouth I'm struck by the thought that I hadn't needed any medication for a long time. I'd been off my antidepressants for awhile, and I never agreed to get back on them. But they're a part of the routine when you enter the mental health unit, the universal cocktail. I swallow the pills with a shot of water, give a mouth check, and turn my back to the door. The trap scares me as it bangs shut. I take the few steps back to my bed and reclaim my place under the blanket. I stare up; "Na-Na loves John 4-eva". I try to focus on just that but my thoughts wander again.

I ruined lives, and I deserve to be in jail, but as I lay on this plastic mattress in the mental health unit, I know that I don't deserve to spend the rest of my life here.

I'm much more than I ever thought I could be. I am a loving person, giving and understanding. I have learned to love myself and others. I have worked hard on my rehabilitation, and I have grown. I earned my GED and learned some skills. I have contributed in many groups and have become a role model for a lot of the younger girls. I pass on my wisdom and knowledge. I have learned to communicate, to express myself, to be an individual, a leader. I have learned so much. I have fully participated in all of the resources available to a woman with the amount of time I'm serving. Now I'm just stagnating.

Because of the length of my sentence, I'm not permitted to take college classes. I am blocked from partaking in other programs because of my sentence. I am only good now for scrubbing down the institution and maintaining its polished floors. I am only good now to shovel out slop in the chow hall and empty the trash. They want me to sweep, mop, and window wash this jail for at least the next thirty-eight years, and I am supposed to choose life over death? I often ask the guards, "Do you remember what you were doing when you were fourteen, or eighteen, or twenty-one, twenty-five, thirty? Can you chart your growth, the lessons you have learned? Can you still laugh at what you once thought was so funny, so important at those ages, but you now know is nonsense? Would you like to wear a scarlet letter on your chest for the rest of your life for the things you did at the age of fourteen? How about a life sentence?"

They stammer and stutter, even the hardest guards admit that it's a mind-blowing concept. I deal with this every day, and that is why I'm wearing this safety gown right now. This is why, occasionally, I can't fathom living this life another day.

I used to feel like a flower that was found dried-out and wilting, ready to die. I was repotted, watered, and cared for until I shed my old petals and bloomed into my beautiful potential. Now that I have flourished and sprouted healthy roots, I need a garden where I can continue to grow. My roots have outgrown this pot, and I am slowly strangling myself. What else am I to do except double back on myself? My growth betrays me as my beauty is wrung from me, a little more each day. I am wasting away in here. This place, this pot, can only take me so far. Don't I deserve a chance to act upon my changes, chase my dreams, reach my goals and live? Now that I have been saved from another attempt on my life, what do I do with that life? This is the last thought on my mind as I look out at the guard perched outside my window. 'Where do I go from here?' This is my last thought as the meds kick in and I drift off to sleep.

'Where do I go from here?'

It is now 2010, a little over two years since my last attempt at suicide. Since then, I have grown even more. I made a promise to myself that I would never again try to end my life and take for granted the blessing God has given me. I am here for a reason.

He has saved me from so many things, including myself, and I realize that now. I have earned my way into two mentoring programs. I am a facilitator in an Alternative to Violence group. I speak with at-risk youth. I have a true spiritual connection with God, and I live in a housing unit that is spiritually based. Some of my writing has been published, and it has given me a voice outside of here and blessed me with new and amazing friends who never let me feel sorry for myself, who push me to do better things.

Just recently, the United States Supreme Court ruled that children under the age of eighteen cannot be given a life sentence if their crime did not result in the death of their victim. That doesn't directly affect me, but it gives me hope. It lets me know that there are people willing to listen and give young offenders a chance at a new and rehabilitated life. It shines a light where darkness once was. I know there is a chance of expanding this law, and it may eventually apply to people like me. I know I will walk out of here one day and be a shining example that people can change. An example that no matter what trauma someone has endured, no matter their family history or their past actions, there is no such thing as a throwaway child.

I am now twenty-eight years old, I have spent the same amount of time in prison as I have on the outside. I have come so far. I will never stop growing.

All I want is a chance to break free from this pot and lay roots in the ground.

GO ON

Spoon Jackson

I cannot go on like this
But I will go on -
on and on, even when
on is off.

Something is stirring
in my soul, wanting
to burst out like
a hot spring in the desert

wanting to come out
and I don't know
what it is - in the moment
I hope it's a poem
I hope it's a song.

Something vast like Euripides
Something wise and funny
like Aristophanes
Something deep like Langston Hughes
So deep in the seas
where no light goes.

I know what it is
I want to create my way
off this lockdown
and write my way
out of prison
They allowed redemption
once, but now only condemnation.

I cannot go on
but I will go on -
on and on even when
on becomes off.

Melancholic and sad
They are letting some
lifers go home
some I have known for a lifetime
and that is a good thing.

Yet there is no end in sight for me
and I don't know
anymore where to go
to get strength to go on.

I don't know where
to go to leave
this sadness and pain
and make my heart sing again
and make my spirit soar again

Everywhere I look
there is a big sign
that says no -

No forgiveness, no love,
no hope, no second chance,
no dreams and no romance.
I cannot go on
but I will go on -
and on and on even when
on becomes off.

But I have nowhere
to go
Nowhere that says
yes.

Yes, it's okay to dream
for some come true
Yes, it's okay to hope
for freedom is free
Yes, it's okay to love
for love can be true.

SLOW DEATH ROW

Patricia Prewitt

"**H**ave a seat, Mrs. Prewitt. I have an idea and want to run it by you," explained my caseworker. I nodded a go-ahead and mentally girded my loins as I settled into the chair across from her desk. Lord only knows what madness this conversation would unleash.

"*I think we should start a cemetery behind 2-House. A graveyard for you and the others serving no-parole.*"

Wow. I sure didn't see that coming. Neither of my feet are even close to, much less in the grave. In fact, I feel pretty good for 50. Or at least I did until she mentioned digging my grave just this side of the fence in the shadows of the razor wire.

"*I'm not talking a huge endeavor since there will only be a few of you who participate, but I'm looking ahead to the geriatric lifer population. You know -- like Ruby, you, Carlene.*"

While she described her vision down to the flower beds and flat gravestones that can be easily mowed over, I sat sad, dumb and numb. It never occurred to me that the state was patiently waiting for me to die, although it makes perfect sense. In their opinion, a pine casket is my only way out, and since I am not directly sentenced to the death penalty, they must wait for me to die on my own. I'm sitting on a painstakingly slow death row.

Ten years later, nothing has come of that caseworker's cemetery idea.

The grass behind our housing unit grows lushly, undisturbed, unlike me, a second-class dead-woman-walking. And there are many thousands just like me in state and federal prisons across our nation.

We are not members of the regular prison population who are encouraged to take classes, learn new work skills, and rehabilitate themselves in preparation for pending reemergence into the free world. But we are not on the formal death row either and therefore have no access to their legislated protections. We are not appointed teams of attorneys who diligently work for reversals. We sentenced to life without the possibility of parole are expected to lay low, stay out of the way, and die as soon as possible to free up some much-needed bed space.

A few years ago I endeavored to reach out and write to every Missouri man locked-up with the same slow death sentence to glean opinions and support for pending legislation. (I already know all the women.) This postage-costly mission opened my eyes to the fact that so many, who have been hopelessly locked up for decades, got in trouble when they were very young. Many are now good people who are truly sorry for the awful mistakes of their misspent youth and are certainly not worthless souls who should be discarded like used Pampers.

We life without the possibility of parole women are no more incorrigible than those serving a fraction of our time. In fact, the prison depends on old lifers to guide and calm the rest. We are the stable, nonviolent mothers of the camp, but we are also women who have been heaved into the landfill of incarceration to rot, not worth the time or trouble to recycle.

Society judges women with a hard eye. If a judge or jury decides we are beyond redemption, there is no reason to look back.

So here I exist at 60, grandmother of 10, still struggling to get the truth out, that the sentence of life without the possibility of parole is a cruel and unnecessary punishment. I pray these truths come to light and are known to be true before that caseworker gets her way and I'm buried out behind the Housing Unit 2 garbage receptacle.

PRISON BLUES

Christian J. Weaver

You don't know loneliness until you're alone
As you don't know death till your name's on a stone
As you haven't seen God with your physical eyes
As you haven't felt grief till your happiness dies.

You don't know loneliness until you're alone
As a wall is a wall till it's also your home
As a fence is a fence till it looks like a cage
As a bird is a bird till it's black as a spade.

You don't know loneliness until you're alone
As you don't know love till your lovers are gone
As you don't perceive fate till it's licking your neck
As you don't adore life till you're sentenced to death.

You don't know loneliness until you're alone
As you don't seek the truth when it's something you know
As you don't see the light till you've bartered your life
For the serum unmixed and the flash of a knife.

MAKING SENSE OUT OF LIFE WITHOUT THE POSSIBILITY OF PAROLE

Dortell Williams

On the inside, within the first layer of ramparts that envelop the gray-walled penal structure, a lethal electrified fence sits that is arguably more gruesome and deadly for its victims than the lofty gun towers that clot the foreboding perimeter. Within the second layer of divisions is a labyrinth of restrictive barriers and brickwork that snake their way toward a larger maze of pavement and chainlink fences that house a virtual world of hardened, concreted, and fortified steel.

The above describes the average purgatorial home for most offenders before they are released back into society. This is also the description of your average permanent house of hopelessness for the fast increasing population of men, women and children forever sentenced to life without the possibility of parole.[1]

This elaborate bulwark of impediments is designed to protect society from the varied collection of denizens sentenced to such hell houses for the crimes they've committed against society. From the non-violent to the extremely violent, their attitudes, temperament and dangerousness to society is about as diverse as the sins they've committed.

It is society's hope that while inside the sinners of society will repent and reform themselves, and that they will conform to societal standards of conduct and become productive, taxpaying members of the law-abiding community.

Unfortunately, the vast majority of penal institutions fail miserably at their calling. Indeed, it is rather a unique aberration for most American "corrections" and "rehabilitation" systems to claim even a reasonable parole-to-success rate. California, by all accounts, has the worst recidivism (return to prison) rate at nearly 70 percent.

California also has one of the largest populations of prisoners sentenced to life without the possibility of parole (3,679), along with Florida (6,424), Louisiana (4,161) and Pennsylvania (4,434). One reason for the increase in life without the possibility of parole sentences, in general, is the failure of penal institutions to rehabilitate prisoners by teaching new skills, ingraining a new mindset, and providing real and tangible post-release support.[2]

Too often prisoners with non-life sentences are released without any meaningful job training or the educational tools necessary to succeed. When they inevitably fail, especially the few who make notorious and tragic mistakes, the news media recycles these stories as if such cases are the norm. The more gruesome the crime, the more sensational the coverage. Understandably, the public is outraged and demands harsher sentences; society wants life "to mean *life*." Unfortunately, the public's ire is then exploited by politicians seeking office or seeking to hold onto their seats. Society is often bewitched by the deception that such crimes of notoriety are the rule, not the exception. Instead of holding wardens accountable, much like teachers are held accountable for their lack of success in the classroom, society's anger is aimed at the hapless prisoner.[3]

America's failed punitive structures have rendered the U.S. shamefully unique among industrialized nations in its arbitrary sentencing schemes. Any objective review of America's draconian sentencing statutes reveals a mishmash of punishments that lack any rhyme or reason. Such a review also illuminates similarities in the lack of value for human life to that of the criminal.

Life without the possibility of parole is nearly unthinkable in other civilized nations. Countries such as Canada, Italy, Mexico, and Peru, among many others, limit incarceration to thirty years.[4] In other countries, when life without the possibility of parole is applied, it is used sparingly. During an address to lawyers in Los Angeles, U.S. Supreme Court Justice Anthony M. Kennedy expressed his dismay at the politicizing of prisons in California stating that U.S. sentences are eight times longer than in European courts.[5]

There is no scientific foundation to America's sentencing patterns. It isn't necessarily how much time an offender serves, but the quality of his incarceration that can determine if he is redeemed or not.[6] This fact is frequently lost in a fog of demagoguery, in the competition to see who can be tougher on crime, in lieu of being smarter, wasting valuable prison space and scarce financial resources.

The politically motivated "tough-on-crime" pursuit is a trend that has, in the past three decades, proven to be a $100 billion farce, its failure indicated by inflated recidivism rates across the land. Life sentences have more than tripled since 1992.[7] States with the largest life without the possibility of parole populations have an average of one out of six prisoners serving these sentences.[8]

The majority of judges frown on removing judicial discretion from other judges through mandatory sentencing. Justice Kennedy criticized California's most influential union, the California Correctional Peace Officers Association (CCPOA), for their role in pushing laws like "three strikes and you're out," characterizing their prison peddling tactics as "sick."[9]

Under California's version of the three-strikes law, an offender convicted of a misdemeanor could be sentenced to twenty-five years to life, the same punishment for murder in the Golden State.

One of the more widely publicized instances of the three-strikes injustice was the case of Gary Ewing, who was sentenced to twenty five years to life for shoplifting three golf clubs from a pro-golf shop.[10] This is the epitome of what Confucius would describe as "using a cannon to kill a mosquito."

The CCPOA is not alone in exploiting prisoners to bolster job security. Many states, such as New York, have relied on prisons for employment.[11] As factory jobs were shipped overseas with little discouragement from lawmakers, a quasi neo-slavery of prisoners took hold. "Build them and they will come," goes the saying. Tweak the policies that lead to prison. Build more prisons. Keeping them filled is the easy part. Longer sentences secure paychecks for prison guards. Never mind the consistent decrease in crime in every state; including those with less punitive measures. Another incentive for local communities to host prisons is a keepsake from slavery's census count of the three-fifths of a person rule. Prisoners counted in modern census undertakings augment the population of the local community, instead of the actual community from which the prisoners come, increasing federal financial support and political representation. American policies incentivize mass incarceration.

It is for these reasons that unions do what they do: promote the growth of prisons for the benefit of their membership.

* * *

On a dark summer night in 1989, I was a twenty-three-year old drug dealer, driving my pregnant twenty-two-year old wife and my two-year-old daughter home. On the way, I decided to make one more drug stop; a decision I'll have to live with for the rest of my life. I was double-crossed and robbed by my associate and his partners, my wife resisted and was mortally shot.

I refused to cooperate with the police because of my culpability in the drug deal. Consequently, I was charged with first-degree murder of my wife, with special circumstances, making me eligible for the death penalty. My wife and I owned a life insurance policy, which the state presented as motive, along with their entirely circumstantial case.

The trial was a seven-month nightmare. The jury deliberated for five long weeks. I was found guilty.

In the penalty phase of the trial, where the panel-of-twelve voted on whether I should live or be put to death, they decided to spare my life. I lost my wife and now I would slowly be put to death, my penalty for choosing the life of a drug dealer.

While I was relieved to live, I was betwixt and between, trapped within the finality of a sentence to be forever lived out in Gehenna's clutches; avoiding the death penalty and losing the right to all of the statutory protections that come with a traditional death sentence. With life without the possibility of parole, absent are the automatic appeals and the close scrutiny that is guaranteed with a death sentence (though incapacitating us for the rest of our natural lives is every bit as serious). To subsist under a life without the possibility of parole sentence still classifies one as a dead man walking, only in slow motion.

Strictly interpreting my case by statute, driving a car made the difference between twenty five years to life and life without the possibility of parole.

Through recent research, I have learned that it was none other than the political maneuvering of the CCPOA itself that created this snare for me and thousands of others. Crime Victims United, created and funded primarily by the CCPOA, helped sponsor the expanding definition of California's special circumstances laws in 1977, 1982, and 1990.[12]

The problem for taxpayers, and the state, is the incredible stress the costs of these inordinately long sentences wreak on other public services, all under the guise of public safety. As Joseph Cassily, past president of the National District Attorneys Association, told USA Today, long prison terms are a "huge drain on resources."[13] Cassily is not alone in his assessment. Susan Nagelsen, a prison reform advocate, writes in the Journal of Prisoners on Prisons that the "growing rate of geriatric prisoners is a looming threat to state expenditures. With elongated sentences, strictly for retributive purposes, not for the more effective rehabilitative process, prisoners are spending longer and longer sentences at state expense, and this population is growing at a rate of ten percent annually."[14]

The Centers for Disease Control in Atlanta, Georgia, estimates an annual cost of $70,000 to treat geriatric-related conditions and diseases.[15] At the outset of proposals for such stretched sentences were prudent fiscal warnings that went unheeded. Gone are the days when I could run around the prison recreation yard for two hours straight, back when I was twenty-three years old. The challenge to contain my hereditary high blood pressure used to be rather effortless, particularly when recreation yard was consistent during the good budget years. Advanced age after twenty-one years in, along with more frequent lockdowns due to staff shortages, and more idle time for fellow prisoners that often lead to incident-related lockdowns, have made the challenge formidable.

The very structure of these houses of horrors wears thin the frame and flesh. The cells are too small for a makeshift alternative to the recreation yard. The limited floor space, barely the size of a small closet, affords little room to stretch, let alone do any meaningful exercise.

Concrete and steel bunks lead to inevitable back problems, the constant stress of prison frays the nerves and raises cortisol levels, which eat away at the circulatory system. Add the natural, inescapable depression that accompanies a hopeless sentence, and health problems are certain. Just this week my new blood pressure pills caused a severe ringing in my ears, which will more than likely require a battery of tests before an alternative medication can be determined.

The prison diet, alone, is detrimental. Almost everything is served from a can, or is otherwise processed, which translates into high-sodium meals laden with PCBs (polychlorinated biphenyl: any of several compounds that are poisonous environmental pollutants which tend to accumulate in animal tissue) certain to kill from consistent and prolonged consumption.

Prison policies also cause our health to decline and health care costs to balloon. Pruno (prisoner-manufactured alcohol) is a popular substance among addicted imbibers. Pruno is made from fruit, usually, but can be composed of just about anything: rice, potatoes, corn, you name it, desperation will find a way. Though the super sippers are a small minority, that fact doesn't restrain the powers that be from all but eliminating fresh fruit from the menu entirely.

I haven't seen an orange or a tomato in over five years. Such policies are contrary to medical wisdom, according to David L. Katz, MD, who recommends men over forty consume at least ten servings of fruit daily.[16] Mass punishment is the penological matter of course which makes the guards' jobs easier and prevails under often cited claims of "safety and security."

The above only touches the surface as to why the sentence of life without the possibility of parole is the other death penalty, and offers graphic elucidation as to the myriad reasons other civilized nations abhor such sentences. Then again, America, unlike other industrialized countries, continues to cling tightly to the ultimate and most irreversible of punishments.

Again, on yet another occasion to critique misdirected U.S. penal policies, Justice Kennedy is not short on criticisms of his home state's penal policies: "It's true that a death sentence is unique in its severity and irrevocability, yet life without the possibility of parole sentences share some common characteristics with death that are shared by no other sentences." "Life without the possibility of parole," Kennedy said, "deprives the convict of the most basic liberties without giving hope."[17]

The sagacious jurist speaks with much insight. Life without the possibility of parole allows an average prisoner to be placed in the general population, but prohibits these men, women, and children from earning their way to lower level prisons for good behavior, almost inciting those with nothing to lose to fall into the most desperate of acts. But, like most lifers, those with life without the possibility of parole are some of the most well-behaved prisoners in the system.

California, arguably one of the worst prison systems in all of the United States, has the highest suicide rate.[18] My guess would be that many of those who attempt or succeed at suicide are lifers, the most hopeless of prisoners. Those of us sentenced to life without the possibility of parole do not have to wait until our forties or fifties to crash into the wall of a mid-life crisis. We are slammed face-first early on when we discover the hopeless reality of these excessive sentences, while similar offenders may still look forward to a future, no matter how distant that future may be. Alexander Cockburn was absolutely correct in his "Dead Souls" article, saying: "What LWOP means is that for the convicted murderers who would otherwise get life with parole, often at very young ages, and who redeem themselves through rehabilitative efforts, even the remotest possibility of release will never become available."[19]

I grew my first beard behind bars. I learned that my natural hair pattern flows to the right in the Los Angeles County Jail. I discovered I had a forte for writing in a four-man cell. Since those early days of self-discovery in my faded youth, I taught myself Spanish with a television and a dictionary, taught myself how to type by sneaking on the clerks' typewriters during their breaks, and earned a paralegal certificate through correspondence.

Later, I was transferred to a pilot program called the Honor Program, initiated by lifers who were tired of the senseless violence, the undercurrent of racism webbed deeply within the fabric of California's prisons, and the rampant drug use. To be eligible, potential participants of the program had to volunteer, vow to abandon any gang ties and drug use, the latter being monitored by random testing, and develop a personal plan for self-rehabilitation.

These and other tenets of the program were written by Kenneth E. Hartman, a man sentenced to life without the possibility of parole as a youth after he killed a man during a fistfight in a drug-fueled, alcoholic stupor that earned him the eternal sentence. Since its inception in 2001, the Honor Program has saved taxpayers millions of dollars, and given the vast majority of lifers in the program a proven track record of rehabilitation.[20]

Through peer-taught classes allowed in the Honor Program I was able to learn how to write professionally under the tutelage of

Hartman. My first nationally distributed article was published by the Christian Science Monitor in 2009, "My Shawshank Redemption."

I have not looked back since.[21] I published the book, *Looking in on Lockdown: A Private Diary for the Public,* and look forward to the release of my next book *Taxpayers, Prisons and Education: The Winners and Losers* this year.

Though frowned upon by my keepers, I have taught myself to operate various computer programs, formed my own writing class to instruct, and earned an Associate of Arts degree in Seminary through a local college. With the limited foresight of youth, I never imagined myself accomplishing such a wide range of activities. I never saw myself as anything more than a drug dealer.

In many ways, such limited personal views are ingrained in youth, particularly those from the inner city. We are told more often what we cannot do than encouraged to find our individual inner gifts. I was told by a high school counselor that I wasn't college material, surely not the first or the last student he disillusioned.

To some degree the naysayers are right in the context of odds. There is a reason inner city children are labeled "at-risk." I surmise it is politically correct not to expound on the label, but to be clear, when they call us "at-risk" they are saying we are at risk of dropping out of school, becoming drug addicts, going to prison, or being completely blotted out. What's amazing is that the structural hurdles that make us at risk are hardly addressed, generation after generation.

During a recent Democratic state attorney general candidate debate, Kamala Harris, then serving as district attorney for San Francisco, pointed out that ninety percent of homicide victims are black, male youth. What's interesting regarding these deadly gang rivalries is that by contrast America spends billions annually to intervene in the centuries-old divide in the Middle East. We spend billions in an attempt to combat piracy on the high seas, driven by poverty in Somalia. We give billions of dollars to Mexico in aid to fight narcotraficantes, but not a measurable fraction of that is directed here to intervene and prevent gang violence.[23]

In spite of comments by the widely revered former Los Angeles Police Chief William Bratton, saying "we cannot arrest our way out of this problem,"[24] we arrest and arrest and arrest, and too many of those arrests result in life without the possibility of parole sentences. The mindset of law enforcement and victims alike is to react, respond, and exact retribution, not prevent, prevail and celebrate the peace. Indeed, the only fundamental difference between a gang banger and a law-abiding citizen, apart from the usual curse of poverty, is the thinking. Change the thinking and you've changed the individual and saved a citizen.

Alberto Terrico, another attorney general candidate, added that we spent more on prisons in 2009 than higher education, a backward trend that urgently needs to be reversed. He further suggested that there is a structured imbalance in funding when, for example, Monterrey schools are funded at $4,700 per student while other venues (insinuating more affluent areas) are granted $7,000 per pupil. Rocky Delgadillo, Los Angeles City Attorney, added that when kids can focus on school they don't have time to get in gangs. Without question, these are structural barriers that invite widespread generational failure and are a built-in threat to public safety.[25]

This is but a brief example of how so many youths end up in prison, of why more than a third of the entire state prison population is harvested and uprooted straight from Los Angeles County, alone.[26]

Assemblyman Ted Lieu, while running for state attorney general, pointed out that six out of ten prisoners are illiterate, yet the prison system allots a mere two percent of its annual $9 billion budget toward rehabilitation programs. Considering that the vast majority of prisoners will eventually be released, this is not conducive to public safety. For Hartman, the technical element that earned him life without the possibility of parole was that he took the victim's wallet and maliciously threw it on the roof. It was that "special circumstance" that separated his crime from say, Robert Jenkins, a man sentenced to twenty-five years to life for the shooting murder of one person and the attempted murder of another.[27] Jenkins can earn his way out of prison if he works hard enough, Hartman cannot.

Is any one murder worse than another? Arguably, Jenkins' state of mind was more malicious than that of Hartman's, for Jenkins' mindset was to kill two people - he simply failed. Yet Hartman is hopelessly restrained after thirty-two consecutive years in prison; a spotless disciplinary record of over twenty years, and an altruistic spirit that has contributed more to curtail prison violence than any other prisoner I know.

Traveille Craig is yet another man involved in a happenstance crime that resulted in an extreme sentence of life without the possibility of parole. In the aftermath of the Rodney King riots, when South Central Los Angeles erupted into mass violence in response to a not guilty verdict for four white officers who were filmed mercilessly beating King, Craig became involved in the contagion of chaos that had maliciously spread to North Hollywood. Craig engaged in a fistfight with another man; the man fell into a coma the night of the fight as a result of a single blow to the head and died eight months later. Craig cooperated with police, and his story was corroborated by the physical evidence. He ended up with life without parole.[28]

These are not the types of crimes for which life without the possibility of parole was created; it was originally introduced as an alternative to the traditional death penalty for serial killers and psychologically deranged offenders who were beyond any possibility of redemption.

Astounding is the absurd assertion that prisoners (implying all) are "hardened" or "incorrigible." Indeed, whenever the majority of people fail in any system, the failing is in the system, not the people. Again, the trend has been to overlook the failed system and punish the hapless prisoner with irrational sentences.

We train dogs and primates to be service animals, to assist and aide the blind and the mobility-challenged.[29] We train dolphins to entertain us and aid law enforcement in anti-terrorism techniques. But we can't rehabilitate people?

People are, in reality, extremely malleable. The military has an extraordinary record of "reforming" people. In fact, when it was U.S. policy to send people accused of crimes to the military, the success rate was the opposite of what our prison failure rates are today. According to a wide-ranging list of sources, statistics show that reformation for lifers is practically automatic. Age, experience, and maturity tend to shear the criminal mindset from most lifers. Not only are lifers historically the most well-behaved in the prison system, they are also the least likely to return to prison once released.[30]

In fact, according to the California Department of Corrections and Rehabilitation's (CDCR) own website, rehabilitation programs such as the California Prison Industry Authority are impressively successful. "CALPIA's Pre-Apprenticeship program is a leading example of how effective rehabilitation reduces recidivism," said Kathy Jett, a spokeswoman for CDCR. CDCR's research showed that participants of CALPIA had a 25 percent lower rate of recidivism than the general population.[31]

In Albuquerque, New Mexico, the correctional system employs charter schools as an avenue for prisoners to earn high school diplomas, which also reduces recidivism rates. With high school dropout rates at nearly 50 percent in some sectors of the nation, this is ideal.[32]

At New York's Christopher Columbus High School in the Bronx, the Council for Unity steers gang members away from the street life and encourages them to hone in on their inner talents. Founded in 1975 by Bob De Sena, a one-time gang member who believes everyone deserves a genuine second chance,[33] not the superficial offerings where a mere two percent of the prisoners have access to meaningful rehabilitation programs.

Deeper still, it's long been forgotten why America adopted the Quaker's version of prison called the "penitentiary." The root word being penitence, the object was to subject the miscreant to a solitary cell with a Bible and let him repent, that is, come to a place of penitence and reform himself. While the specific results of that experiment left a murky history, it is obvious that the aim and ideal of the Quakers has been corrupted and subverted. As mentioned earlier, profit and political motives have filled the cells to overflowing, prohibiting any prisoner from "finding himself" in the chaotic ruckus of the prison environment we have today. The modern American prison offers prisoners nothing more than an idle, purposeless setting to be physically warehoused and mentally stagnated. Prisoners revolve in and out of prison doors with increasing costs to state coffers, increased victimization, with mandatory life sentences ridiculously stacked one upon another culminating in the world's largest prison population.

As is often cited by prison reformers: *America comprises just 5 percent of the world's population but hosts 25 percent of its prisoners.* While it is obvious that the U.S. is at odds with the rest of the world in its approach to punishment and human reform, Vernor Munoz, Special Rapporteur on the Right to Education, an independent expert appointed in 2008 by a body of the United Nations, had this to say about modern criminal justice, prisoners, and education: "Opportunities for education should be commonplace in detention, not simply an add-on should resources 'allow' it. It should be aimed at the full development of the whole person requiring, among others, prisoner access to formal and informal education, to literacy programmes, basic education, vocational training, creative, religious and cultural activities, physical education and sport, social education, higher education, and library facilities."[34]

Munoz further offers: "The challenge before us is to create an environment for those who are detained that enables human dignity, capacity, and positive change."[35] We have a choice what model of prisons we wish to facilitate and pay for.

Once the process of personal reform is claimed by any prisoner, and their minimum time served, a parole board reviews, screens, and measures that claim. Prisoners trying to convince a parole board that they've been rehabilitated face a formidable challenge. According to Scott Handleman, an attorney in San Francisco who represents prisoners in parole hearings, there were 31,051 prisoners serving life with parole in California in 2008, with 8,815 of those having been incarcerated beyond their minimum eligibility release dates, and out of that number 6,272 prisoners went before the parole board. A mere 272 prisoners were found suitable for parole dates. Under California law, the governor must review parole board recommendations, consequently politicizing the process. In 2007, between .01 and .02 percent of those found suitable by the parole board were approved by the governor's review.[36]

Second chances for lifers are virtually nonexistent.

For those sentenced to life without the possibility of parole, there is no second chance, virtual or otherwise. The parole board is prohibited from even reviewing such cases. They will never hear about the rehabilitation success stories of prisoners like Hartman and Craig and the many others just like them.

This makes no sense at all.

To the rest of the world America's justice system is notorious for its three-strikes law, life without the possibility of parole and other mandatory sentences. Our country sentences and imprisons its citizens with less humanity than the Third World countries it condemns for their gross human rights violations.

Let us review the closing statement of Vernor Munoz's report:

> Deprivation of liberty should be a measure of last resort. Given the considerable negative long-term economic, social and physiological consequences of detention on detainees, their families and the community, considerably greater attention should be paid to implementing alternatives to detention for children and adults alike.[37]

This makes sense to me.

Sources:

[1] Ashley Nellis and Ryan S. King, "No Exit: The Expanding Use of Life Sentences in America," July 2009: p.3

[2] ibid., pp. 3, 3-9

[3] Kristine Torres, "Vote Pits Teachers Against Governor," <u>Atlanta Journal Constitution</u>, April 27, 2010: B1

[4] <u>USA Today</u>, "Van der Sloot Disclosure Reverberates," June 9, 2010: 6A

[5] Carol J. Williams, "Justice Kennedy Laments the State of Prisons in California, U.S." <u>Los Angeles Times</u>, February 4, 2010

[6] Coleman et al. v. Schwarzenegger; Plata et al. v. Schwarzenegger; Perez et al. v. Tilton; <u>www.cdcr.ca.gov/communications/prisonover crowding.html</u>

[7] Ashley Nellis and Ryan S. King, "No Exit: The Expanding Use of Life Sentences in America," July 2009: p.2

[8] ibid., pp. 5-9

[9] <u>The New York Times</u> [Editorial], "Justice Kennedy on Prisons," February 16, 2010

[10] ibid.

[11] Martha T. Moore, "Jobs Lost as States Close Prisons," <u>USA Today</u>, August 18, 2009,

[12] Proposition 18 (SB 1878 of the 1997-98 Reg. Session) Murder: Special circumstances; Legislation Initiative Amend.; Proposition 7 (SB 155, 1997); Propositions 114 and 115 in 1990; Proposition 196 enacted by the voters in 1996, explaining the number of special circumstances

[13] Kevin Johnson, "Report Pushes Abolishing Life Without the Possibility of Parole Sentences," <u>USA Today</u>, July 23, 2009

[14] Susan Nagelsen, Journal of Prisoners on Prisons (2006) Vol. 14:2, pp. v-x

[15] ibid.

[16] John Brant, "Look Great at Any Age," Men's Health, pp. 146 (quoting Dr. Katz)

[17] USA Today, "Life Without Deprives the Convict of the Most Basic Liberties W/O Giving Hope," May 18, 2010

[18] Don Thompson (AP), "California Inmate Suicides Climb, Security Changes Blamed," (August 6, 2005 harold.com); cdcr.ca.gov; Coleman, et al.

[19] Alexander Cockburn, "Dead Souls," Counterpunch, May 8-10, 2009

[20] Kenneth E. Hartman, "Mother California: A Story of Redemption Behind Bars", (Atlas & Co., 2009); www.kennethehartman.com.

[21] dortellblogs.blogspot.com

[22] ibid.

[23] Democratic State Attorney General Candidate Debate, KABC-7, May 23, 2010

[24] William Bratton, "We Can't Arrest Our Way..." KTLA-5 News, June 3, 2004

[25] Democratic State Attorney General Candidate Debate, KABC-7, May 23, 2010

[26] California Department of Corrections and Rehabilitation, "Corrections / Moving Forward," (33% of prison pop. emanates from L.A. County) (2009) p.11

[27] People v. Jenkins, 19 Cal. Rptr. 3d 386 (the name Robert is fictional)

[28] Travielle Craig, CDCR# H98882; Superior Court No. LAO12897, Van Nuys Superior Court RT 2, p. 462 (Dr. Sathyavagiswaran's testimony); RT 1, p. 193 (Confession tapes); RT 1, p. 8 (Craig only struck victim once); RT 1, p.17 (Craig cooperated with police)

[29] USA Today, "Vermont Allows Monkeys Trained as Service Anima|s," June 3, 2010, 3A

[30] Wilbert Rideau and Ron Wikberg, "Life Sentences: Rage and Survival Behind Bars," (Times Books, NY, NY 1992) pp. 67-68; National Council on Crime and Delinquency, 1965-1969; Sentencing Project (www.sentencingproject.org)

[31] Convict News, "Rehab Programs Lead to Jobs and Lower Recidivism," February 2009, p. 35; cdcr.ca.gov.

[32] Heather Clark, "Charter Schools Help Inmates Earn High School Diplomas," Antelope Valley Press, January 2, 2009, B3, Associated Press

[33] Ula llnytzky (AP) "Group Turns Gangsters into College Students," Christian Science Monitor, March 3, 2008, p.1

[34] Vernor Munoz, "The Right to Education of Prisoners in Detention: Summary of Report Presented to the UN Human Rights; Committee in June 2009 (Journal of Prisoners on Prisons, Vol. 18, No. 1 & 2, 2009) p. 165

[35] ibid.

[36] Alexander Cockburn, ibid.

[37] Vernor Munoz, "The Right to Education of Prisoners in Detention: Summary of Report Presented to the UN Human Rights Committee in June 2009 (Journal of Prisoners on Prisons, Vol. 18, No. 1 & 2, 2009) p. 165

TOO CRUEL, NOT UNUSUAL ENOUGH

Joseph A. Badagliacca

I never said I didn't deserve *some* type of punishment. Even as a kid you know if you do something wrong there are consequences. Things tend to happen though. You blink and when you open your eyes you truly wish you had the ability to turn back time.

But now, as I sit here and write, I can't concentrate on rewinding the clock, I have this damn contraption locked to my arm. I don't know if you've ever seen the likes of this. Picture an intravenous tube, bolted to the crook of the arm, around the elbow area. The tube dangles down like a tentacle that has a mind of its own. It is definitely not removable, believe me I've tried. The court must have ordered it attached to my arm while I was sleeping. They did a good job because no matter what I try, it is not coming off. It was on my arm when I woke up the day after my murder trial concluded. Obviously, I was found guilty and the replay of those unfathomable words keeps playing in my mind: *'life without the possibility of parole, life without the possibility of parole ...'*

This tube has become unbearable, tangling with my arm and wrist with each movement of the pen across this paper. It bears resemblance to a medical drip, but it works in reverse. It has a vacuum that siphons my spirit from me with each breath I take. I hold my breath, and it slows the flow of my spirit, but I still see it exiting my body. There is no stopping the systematic flow and, at times, it causes me to hyperventilate as I'm gripped by the reality of this horror. It's pretty creepy, to say the least.

They don't know it, but I have an old sort of life support system I keep hidden in my cell. I use it sparingly when no one else is around. This system provides me with small doses of what I call Hope to help ease the pain of the contraption. Don't make me go into the technical details, it's really a personal experience that at least provides a little relief - even if it's only a temporary fix. Seriously though, I don't know what I'd do without it.

The contraption attached to my arm has the inscription *Deathbed* and is surprisingly light and mobile. I function as normally as one possibly can, given my condition. I go to work six days a week, pretty much all day, at the prison law library and assist others as best as I can with this thing clouding my thoughts. I don't get paid to work, but the daily routine has a semblance of normalcy to it. People tend to ignore this ridiculous monstrosity drooping from my arm.

My "condition" prohibits me from obtaining any vocational training or higher education because they tell me I am considered a "security threat." This results in the monotony of knowing I am never going to progress, never going to better myself, never going anywhere. . . *ever*. I have to stop thinking like that, it makes the *Deathbed* drain faster.

Anyways, as I was saying, the monotony of work helps me to forget the fact that I am dying with each and every breath I take. After work, I come back to my cell and sit for a few moments with my life support system trying to squeeze out a little Hope to ease the reality. Using the system is difficult because Hope is so fleeting.

On visits, Mom holds my hand as I lay in my *Deathbed.* I know she has no clue what to do. She cries and prays to God for us to find the tools to remove the tube. Sometimes, after I use the Hope system, and it takes effect, I can talk to her about freedom, or fishing, walking, eating a decent meal, and just living, instead of the dying, always the dying. Then the effect of the system starts to fade, along with my Hope, and we're back to her not knowing what to say. So she says anything, but thankfully she refuses to mention the obvious deterioration she sees in me day after day. She is the only one who comes. I guess because people are afraid that it's contagious, or they can't stand the sight of me in my *Deathbed*. Looking at the toll it's taking on her, I'd say it might actually *be* contagious.

The guys I'm around, for the most part, don't understand my death sentence. I can't say *I* understand it half the time. But it's difficult for them to imagine because they're getting out some day, or they have a chance for parole, however slim that chance may be. But, *it is a chance.*

The doctors have given me the grim diagnosis that I am as healthy as a thirty-three year old can be. So, unfortunately for me (and those paying for the *Deathbed*) this process could conceivably take another fifty or so years. It's been attached to my arm going on fourteen years now, and there seems no chance that this thing is going to malfunction or be removed by clemency or commutation.

I've scratched, and I've clawed, and I've pulled; nothing works.

After all this time, I'm at a point in my death where there is little to do but watch life simply fade away. I've accomplished what little I'm allowed to in here. I earned my G.E.D., law certificate, and my ESL tutoring certificate. I've begun to question why I even bother. My life support system is getting too weak to provide the necessary Hope I need to continue on. I've been using the system so much and for so long that I'm no longer able to distort the reality of my sentence. Who knows if the system will even start up the next time I try.

The incision where the tube extends from my arm is starting to itch again. It does that when I try to do anything constructive. I really don't have much incentive to be productive nowadays anyway. It's all just a relentless cycle, like that movie "Groundhog Day" where Bill Murray's character wakes up to the same day over and over and over.

There are many times when I genuinely envy those to whom the court just flat out said, "We are going to kill you." Those guys, at least, have a shorter wait for the inevitable; a set date to die. I wonder if they look at my *Deathbed* and say, "Thank God the court didn't do *that* to me," or maybe not. To each his own cross to bear, they say. But at least the tubes used on those guys kill them as quickly and humanely as killing someone can be. I thought *any* death penalty was not allowed to be torture. I see I was wrong.

Well, I have been as productive as I can be today. My arm is itching and aggravating me worse than normal. I am going to try to get my system to start up, I need a good dose of Hope today. I'll sure be happy the day Mom can release my hand and know my suffering has ended because then I'll know hers has ended, too. For loving me she has been suffering her own penalty.

If you find this letter and I am unconscious, see if *you* can find a way to get this thing off my arm. I'd be thankful beyond words, because I know I could succeed at living a productive life in society if I was given the chance. I think a lot of people believe in second chances. Too bad whoever put this on my arm doesn't. There is no way in the world that they can see what these *Deathbeds* are doing. They can't see that they are too cruel, and without a doubt, not unusual enough.

TOO CRUEL A FATE

Kenneth E. Hartman

I've already missed too many of the big milestones of her life. She came into the world without me being there to watch her fall into this world. Her first steps happened while I was locked securely away serving life without the possibility of parole. She went off to her first day of school, came home from her first dance recital, and went to bed waiting for the tooth fairy's nocturnal visit without me.

She arrived back when California still thought that all prisoners should be able to spend a couple of days of private time with their families in little apartments on prison grounds. Her mother and I were crazy in love, and we both fantasized that parenthood could work even if I remained in prison. We also labored under the delusion I wasn't actually going to spend all my remaining days locked up. The idea that the state would exact a punishment of forever didn't seem likely; it didn't seem real. Even now, after all this time, there remains a surreal quality to this death penalty.

She's a teenager now, with all that portends. I wasn't around to teach her how to ride a bicycle, and I'm not there now to teach her how to drive. More importantly, I can't be standing at the front door to size up the young men who'll come calling and, thus, won't be able to afford to her the benefit of my experience and discernment.

When I was but a few years older than she is now, a teenager filled with irrational anger and the boundless, unbounded energy of youth,

I took offense at a few words of insult. I beat a 44-year-old man to death in a little park surrounded by the streets I'd walked and skateboarded since I was a boy. Fueled by the unhappiness of my childhood, and supercharged in the rage-inducing mix of tequila and methamphetamine, I poured my misery out onto a poor homeless man.

Though all of this happened lifetimes ago, and I have to strain against the fog of forgetting that obscures everything that took place so far off and long ago, I understand ever more clearly how wrong my actions were that cool February night.

What I denied to Thomas Alan Fellowes is now denied to me. In fundamental ways, I ended both of our lives that misbegotten night. Whatever possibilities stretched out before us closed down securely, ineradicably.

It's true that one could argue I've still carved a kind of life out of my isolation. I married, fathered a child, published a book, and I'm deeply involved in a number of useful projects, not least of which is the movement to end the other death penalty, life without the possibility of parole. But I'm the exception to the dismal reality of this sentence.

Most of my peers never receive a single visit, not from their families or friends, and certainly not from the children they never had. Instead, they languish in a tortured twilight world between life and death. And this fate isn't reserved for a few super-criminals, mass murderers, or drug kingpins; it's the sentence of more than 41,000 men, women, and children. It's unprecedented, too, in the long course of human history, as nowhere in the past, and nowhere now in the present, in any other country in the world, were or are people sentenced to the rest of their lives in prison.

What happened to cause this negative paradigm shift is a troubling case of many factors coalescing, among them the industrialization of incarceration, the terrible, wrongheaded decision to bargain with the executioners using the chip of this other death penalty, and the manipulation of the public into a near-constant state of terror by self-serving politicians and the voracious, soulless media. Deeper, though, something much more profound and tragic happened to this country.

Americans, by and large, lost faith in humanity and embraced a strange kind of materialistic nihilism. Things became more important than people, as people devolved into lesser things. This is evident in the frightening march of the past 25 years to bury ever-younger children under longer and longer sentences, to the ways public employee unions representing prison guards lobby shamelessly to keep more people in prison for longer periods of time regardless of the vast collateral damages to families and communities, to the trumpeting of abusive jail and prison conditions that results in general approval by the public and the reelection of blowhard bullies to endless terms of office. It's a shameful spectacle.

Life without the possibility of parole is the ultimate anti-human prison sentence, even more than the traditional execution, which as an act of pure revenge is really not a commentary on the worth of the criminal, only on the severity of the crime. The other death penalty, by contrast, is a statement of condemnation against even the mere possibility a person might, someday in the future, manage to struggle against the odds and become better than their worst moment. It is a sentence that posits, as its underpinning, that in no amount of time or consequent to any degree of concerted effort could an offender achieve rehabilitation or reform sufficiently enough to warrant consideration of another chance in the world on the other side of the fences.

The death penalty abolition movement, more interested in achieving results than pursuing truth, fell prey to the bogus logic that sentencing men and women to die in prison isn't a death sentence. More cynically, they recruited the uglier side of the victims' rights movement to bolster their position, adopting as good policy the lifetime-of-suffering model of corrections. Instead of working to educate the public about why modern civilized countries shouldn't execute people, they took the low road and appealed to the idea that the other death penalty is actually an economical execution.

It's more vengeance and retribution without the excessive costs and troublesome sociopolitical aspects of lethal injections – a dance with Mephistopheles that is the proximate cause of the exponential growth in the other death row. And, surely, a poor bargain that will result in worse troubles down the line, long after the limousine lefties have stopped patting themselves on their collective back for being so clever at outsmarting the unsophisticated guards' unions and ignorant crime victims' groups.

Actually, those "unsophisticated" guards couldn't love a sentence more than life without the possibility of parole. It's all about job security, as they'll readily admit in here out of earshot of the gullible public. Those of us sentenced to death by imprisonment have created a lot of very well paid jobs and, as the years progress and we get older and far more expensive, we'll continue to provide a heavy keel for this bloated system.

Because life inside prison is, in fact, a horrific existence filled with endless stress and misery, the incidence of chronic, age-related diseases skyrockets amongst older prisoners. We are sclerotic, arthritic, and cancerous far more than people on the other side of the fences of the same age. We older prisoners are much more expensive and less well equipped than the younger men these places were originally designed to hold. The stairs are too steep, the beds too high, and the floors and walls too hard for old, brittle bones. Security procedures that made some kind of sense to restrict rambunctious twentysomethings are simply ridiculous and excessive when applied to tottering 60 and 70-year-olds. This applies no less to the whole concept of endless incarceration than to transporting feeble old folks to chemotherapy treatments in ten pounds of stainless steel shackles with multiple layers of armed guards.

Little of this analysis makes much of a difference to the unhappiness of a teenaged daughter permanently denied the presence of her father. For her, it all boils down to the loss of any possibility of ever seeing her father as a complete man. Never will I be on the scene, standing beside her, lending her a shoulder to lean on in the storms that pass through every life.

The determination of my inability to ever be able to safely function again in society took place when I was 19 years old. And it simply must be based on the safety-to-others standard, at least that's the socially utilitarian fiction behind which the system of mass incarceration hides. Otherwise, all of this, the edifice of imprisonment that's gobbling up the other more useful functions of government, is nothing more than a modernized pillory, a newer, less appalling stocks, a sanitized gibbet. Of course, the gorier truth beyond the slogans is this is the place where, instead of displaying the rotting corpses of executed criminals swinging above the town square, society hides them away, out of view, to slowly wither away and expire, quietly, cleanly.

That's how the prison-industrial complex so effectively and deftly managed to outmaneuver the smarty-pants death penalty abolitionists. Being in the business of dealing with the worst, smallest aspects of human nature, the boss-men saw their best play was to erect a wall of fear and loathing between prisoners and the rest of the world. They knew the desire for revenge is deep and easily piqued by a tearful mother, a bereft child, or the haunting specter of the monstrous, the remorseless, the serial killer, the inhuman brute who kills without thought.

The marketing campaign that sold the idea of expanding the use of the other death penalty is a remarkable study in how to sell two sides of a counterfeit coin at the same time. It's the most perfect example of talking out of both sides of the mouth. Life without the possibility of parole is vigorously pushed as what it is – a capital punishment, the end of a life. This is done to satisfy the hang 'em high folks who would like to see the kid who stole their car drawn and quartered in the town square. (And there are, for the record, a large number of prisoners serving life without the possibility of parole who did not kill anyone. The prison-industrial complex, ever eager to secure more stable cargo in its hold, promotes the idea that nothing speaks more loudly about "getting tough" than sentencing young men and women to the slow death of a lifetime of imprisonment.)

On the other side of the coin, out of the other side of the mouth as it were, life without the possibility of parole is soft-pedaled as a nicer kind of death penalty; an execution without all of the messy, unpleasant aspects of the traditional version. The innocent can be exonerated, they love to exalt, neglecting to mention that the other death penalty does not carry with it the automatic, high-powered attorneys of the traditional version. It's actually a lot less likely that an innocent will be freed from this other death row.

It'll cost less than traditional executions is another selling point for the push to expand life without the possibility of parole. The trouble with this analysis is it's all front-loaded. The big costs for the other death penalty come at the back end when old prisoners start to come undone, as all old people are wont to do. It's just that when old prisoners start to fall apart they do it in a spectacularly expensive fashion.

The naked heart of the position advocating for life without the possibility of parole as a reasonable alternative revolves around the argument of which kind of execution is more humane. The idea of going through all of the grotesqueries of performing a traditional execution repels many people, as it should. Last meals, visits from soft-spoken, somber clergy, the last desperate hug from a grieving mother or the stolen kiss from a soon-to-be widow, all of these images leave a bad taste. And the actual act, the strapping down of a human being to a frighteningly cruciform, antiseptically sterile examination table, the application of adhesive electrodes to monitor heart and brain function, the insertion of the needle into the arm or leg, and the drawing open of curtains for the viewers seated in orderly rows behind large panes of spotless glass – it's all a surreal theater of the absurdly brutal. The death-inducing chemicals are anti-climactic, rendering the extermination of a human, the deliberate, premeditated homicide for the sole, expressed purpose of revenge and retaliation, an affair of disappointing, picayune regulations performed by lowly functionaries. The victims, for whom this *danse macabre* is performed, never speak of achieving their promised, longed for "closure." This is the modern death penalty, exacted on mostly poor and minority men in the dead of night.

No one could argue that's a humane way for the state to conduct its business, at least no one whose thinking has evolved out of the 18th century. But the argument that trading the horror show just described for life without the possibility of parole constitutes a step up or a step forward is not accurate.

A prisoner sentenced to the other death penalty can look forward to serving the rest of his or her life in the worst prisons in the country. The worst prisons in this country are bad in ways the average citizen cannot really comprehend because of all the "country club" propaganda spread by the angriest victims' groups and the pandering politicians of the past generation.

American prisons are the worst in the industrialized world and often sink down to Third World conditions. Violence, both from other prisoners and at the hands of guards, is rampant. Sexual assault is commonplace, tolerated, and built right into the macho culture of prison. Medical and dental care runs from rudimentary to criminally nonexistent, and mental health services are tantamount to a bad joke. Even though enormous sums of money are allocated to care for prisoners, because the "caregivers" tend to view their "patients" as little more than irritating scum it's about as useful as pouring money down a drain to unclog the pipes. Prisoners spend most of their time under some form of lockdown, which translates into no out-of-cell time for weeks to months save the occasional shower. Food is atrocious, recreation is sparse to nonexistent, and opportunities to participate in meaningful programs are rare, at best.

And, as bad as spending 30, 40, even 50 years or more under these conditions may sound, in contrast to the traditional death penalty, a sentence of life without the possibility of parole brings with it no special protections, no high-profile supporters, and no high-minded legal representation.

Prisoners sentenced to the traditional form of execution are always held in separate units away from the general population of the prison. In times past, this translated down to horrible conditions of isolation and abuse. Generally speaking, with the overall deterioration of conditions throughout American prisons, it is now probably true that the various death rows have become safer and less abusive than the rest of the prison system.

Prisoners sentenced to the other death penalty, by contrast, are deliberately and permanently housed in the most violent, most repressive prisons. It's in these overcrowded pressure cookers of racism, rape, and brutality that those condemned to death by imprisonment spend the rest of their lives.

All across the country, out in front of every prison with a death house, supporters of the condemned hold marches and protests. They sing songs and light candles, holding up photos of those scheduled to be killed by the state. It's a touching testament to the good of some in the face of the brutality of others. Inevitably, big footprint celebrities show up to offer their star power to the efforts. In the famous newspapers and on the prestigious websites they write about how morally wrong it is to conduct such barbaric rituals, about how it's time to move forward as a modern civilization. They regularly point out the relatively enlightened stance of our peer countries, virtually all of which have long abandoned traditional executions.

Curiously, these great defenders of the March of Progress never mention that our better allies also don't use life without the possibility of parole. In fact, many countries in our democratic coalition believe that death by imprisonment is also an unacceptably harsh and inhumane penalty. Some won't extradite one of their citizens to this country if they face either form of the death penalty.

Out in front of the hundreds of maximum-security prisons that blight the rural landscape of this country and that hold the more than 41,000 men, women, and children sentenced to the long, slow death penalty of life without the possibility of parole, there are no rallies, no moving speeches, and never any famous faces challenging the public to abandon these retrograde forms of punishment. Usually, the reverse is true. The famous progressives, in their wound-up, overwrought, emotional opinion pieces invariably offer up the other death penalty as the fair and reasonable compromise.

As to the legal situation, there is a virtual army of top-notch lawyers who comprise the cream of the criminal defense crop vigorously representing those sentenced to the traditional form of the death penalty. It's an industry. Appeals to the highest courts are automatic and all the legal guns are brought out to pursue them to the fullest extent. Death penalty appeal lawyers are a special branch of the legal world, filled with the zeal of a calling to fight against what is, indeed, an inherently unjust sentence. A social stratum that agrees on the need to change this wrong also funds them, and quite well. They knock down doors and put boots to recalcitrant butts in their forceful attempts to spring their clients from the executioners' grasp.

Life without the possibility of parole doesn't attract the same kind of passion or the same level of funding. The other death penalty is the poor stepbrother, legally. There are no enhanced protections that bring about the heightened scrutiny of traditional death sentences, and there are no well-heeled lawyers showing up with hardnosed investigators ready to turn over every stone in pursuit of justice. There are no university law school programs dedicated to freeing the innocent men and women sentenced to the other death penalty, let alone abolishing this equally unjust sentence.

The fact of the matter is society made a collective decision to accept as right and proper condemning tens of thousands to die slowly in prison. Outside a relatively small circle of activists and a few mostly obscure legal scholars, life without the possibility of parole is settled law and policy. And absent some truly radical changes to the criminal law statutes of the 49 states that use life without the possibility of parole, the number populating the other death row will continue to grow. It took about a quarter of a century to get to this point; it'll take far less time to reach 100,000 human beings sentenced to no parole, no hope, and no possibility.

Inevitably, the question will arise about the philosophy of just deserts, or as it's more commonly framed, "You should have thought about all of this before you killed somebody." I can't argue about the literal point. I should have, but I didn't. If I could go back in time and counsel myself when I was a 19-year-old, I certainly would. But I can't. The real lead to this story, and the tens of thousands of others like it, is life without the possibility of parole freezes someone into their worst moment forever. It denies the hope of positive growth and change that's oxygen for the spirit of all human beings. More than 30 years ago a judge made a decision to prevent me from ever earning parole because I couldn't change for the better. But I did.

My time serving this other death penalty has worn me down. The decades of living on the frontlines of the struggle to halt and reverse the coarsening and worsening of the biggest prison system in the country knocked holes in my physical being. I've been put in the hole several times, once at the behest of the former Secretary of Corrections himself, for daring to speak out, for having the temerity to challenge the slide into madness that is the direction of the prison system. I take cold comfort in the exoneration of my contentious assertions by multiple courts and numerous boards and commissions. From in here, the progress down the path to certain chaos and oblivion appears to continue, unchecked. From in here, the great engine of the gigantic and all-powerful prison-industrial complex appears to remain well defended inside an impregnable fortress.

I tell my daughter, when she asks me the dreaded when-will-this-end question, I don't know the answer. It would be heartless to tell her I fear my only way out is the proverbial pine box.

Nevertheless, as long as I draw breath and possess my wits, I'll continue to take a leadership role trying to make the system better. Because I'll never have to perform the awkward buck dance in front of a slanted, hostile parole board, I have a freer hand to speak truth to power, to call attention to the rotten stench that permeates the air in these places. If nothing else, at least my daughter can take some solace in the fact that her father was willing to stand up for what is right, even when the cost was painfully steep.

And, in my heart of hearts, I truly believe that life without the possibility of parole, the other death penalty, will ultimately be abandoned, along with all other forms of the death penalty, by our country. I like to imagine this leap forward will take place before I've left this plane of existence for whatever awaits me in the hereafter, but of that I'm not overly optimistic. I realize it's going to take an enormous amount of educating the public as to what the prison-industrial complex has been up to these past decades.

It's also going to require a massive organizing effort that simply must include prisoners serving the other death penalty. On the ground, on the yard, this means that those of us who understand what's been going on, how we've all been used and duped, need to convince our brothers and sisters it's time to stop biting into the stupidity of prison. We who will always be here need to work together to create spaces inside the system where sanity, healing, and useful productivity can flourish.

Odds are, I won't be able to participate in any of the most significant moments of my daughter's life. I know this sad truth all too well. But, no matter how many times I try to understand the bigger picture, it still doesn't make any sense to me, not after all these years, not after the exhaustion of any logical basis for making me sit here waiting to die.

It seems, simply, too cruel a fate.

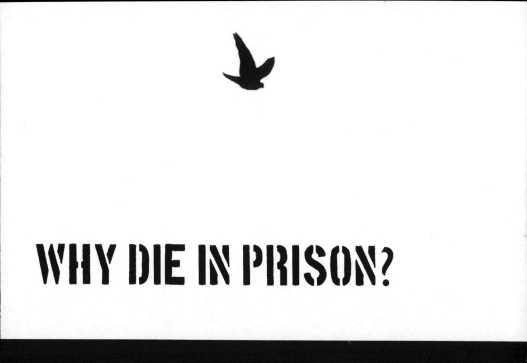

S ure, being tough on crime sounds like a good idea. "Let's make them all pay!" It's easy for a politician or a public official to say something along these lines. And why wouldn't they? It seems like it makes sense to be as tough as possible toward criminals to prevent crime. So when the idea of a life sentence that didn't offer parole came along, everyone was on board. "It'll be a great deterrent," was the mantra on the policymakers' lips. Problem is, it isn't working. Instead, it produced a sentence that's basically the death penalty because the person is sentenced to die in prison; and a rapidly growing population is serving this death sentence.

For people like myself, who have been sentenced to life without the possibility of parole at a young age (eighteen in my case), there is a chance we will be in prison for sixty or more years. By giving me this sentence, the state has implied that I am an errant far beyond any means of rehabilitation, even after a period of thirty or forty years. If the state cannot rehabilitate a person after such a long period of time, then that is more of an indictment on the state's capabilities.

The life without the possibility of parole sentence is purely a revenge sentence. Shouldn't I at least be given the chance to prove myself to society? Instead, I was given a sentence that will result in my death in the custody of the state. A death sentence. A sentence of death. Only instead of having a needle full of poison stuck in my arm,

I'm expected to grow old and eventually expire. Same as on a driver's license, I'm just a number that will eventually expire.

Instead of attempting to guess at a person's sentencing hearing how they're going to act and what their mindset will be twenty or thirty years in the future, why not use existing methods to monitor these factors throughout a person's sentence? There is a parole board set up for this very purpose. If a person is uncooperative or doesn't want to work toward release, then the state has the option of not granting parole. In so doing, the state can effectively keep somebody in prison with the possibility of parole as if they had a life without the possibility of parole sentence. Removing certain death by incarceration would not impact the state's ability to keep dangerous people locked up. But for those who seek healing and restoration, they should be able to work toward it and earn it.

For example, let's say somebody is sentenced to life without the possibility of parole and acts out because he feels he has nothing to lose. The state will argue that this is proof that they sentenced him correctly because of his continued behavioral problems; however, had the person at least the chance for parole, he might not have acted out, he may even have become a model prisoner. He might have become a good citizen. Instead, the life without the possibility of parole sentence became a self-fulfilling prophecy.

Instead of putting the nails in the coffin twenty or thirty years too soon, shouldn't there at least be a chance to work toward restoration? The parole board should be the entity that decides, at the appropriate time, whether or not someone is to be paroled or whether he will die in prison. The reasons are already there to change the sentencing system, now there needs to be the will.

THINKING OF YOU

Robert C. Chan

The inmates milled about the dayroom. Four-seater stainless steel tables shaped like stop signs held games of pinochle, poker, and dominoes. Another table had a couple of guys pouring over a Black's Law Dictionary, manually typed writs and briefs splotched with chunky white-out were arranged in neat stacks. At yet another table the old man stood beside his makeshift greeting card stand. Everyone referred to him as "the old man," but addressed him as "youngster." I called him Hal. That's the name he gave me when we met that night, when I first arrived here, seven years ago.

He stood there with his cards set up on the table, cards for every occasion. I browsed through a few, not really in the market to purchase – since I have no one to send a card to – I was just curious. I noticed the cards were recycled, the inner parts skillfully replaced with new paper; and none of them was accompanied by its original factory envelope; all of the envelopes were homemade, expertly folded, sharply creased, even flourished with a gummed strip for sealing – yet homemade, just the same. Priced at 50¢, half the price of the cards sold in the commissary, I agreed to pay two ramen soups for a "thinking of you" card I didn't need. I'm not sure why I did that, just something about the old man made me want to do something nice. The strange thing is, it was with profound kindness and compassion that Hal said to me, "Everything's gonna be alright, son."

Eventually I was assigned to work here in the housing unit, sweeping, mopping, basic janitorial duty. This afforded the opportunity to become better acquainted with Hal. Hal enjoyed watching his old Zenith in his cell. Turning the television on often reminded him of his old buddy, John. John, who "couldn't wire a light for shit, nor fix electrical outlets," was assigned to the technician/electrician's department. What John did do was pester the Administration till they installed an analog-to-digital converter on the institution's main antenna to pipe the signal to all the cells. Hal couldn't afford an upgrade. For several months after the big FCC switchover, he had to go without his beloved PBS programs. When the converter was finally installed it was once again the joys of Frontline, Globe Trekker, and Hal's favorite – The Antiques Road Show. John never saw the benefits of the new digital signal, his old ticker stopped ticking two days before.

John, like Hal, was an L-WOP, which means he was serving a life without the possibility of parole sentence. But John did get paroled, even if it was with a tag on his toe. I never learned exactly what John did to get here. Hal killed a man in a drunken brawl. Forty years later you could hear the remorse, the sadness etched in his voice as he told the story of how a young fool, just like himself, ended up dead in a fistfight, when it could just as easily have been Hal.

It seems Hal had been trying to make amends ever since. Equipped with an easy smile and a kind word, he did what he could to help newcomers adjust to prison life. He often shared the meager profits of his greeting card venture; some toothpaste, a ramen soup, a shot of coffee, these things can go a long way to help a guy over the hump. Hal was generous with his time, as well. He'd tutor basic education if you were seriously committed to learning. He signed up and was accepted to work in the caregivers program, providing aid for mostly bedridden inmates diagnosed with "less than a year to go." He'd hoped for a pay number, but the economy didn't permit the state to create any more 8¢-an-hour inmate salaries. Early on he'd been tempted to quit and try for a job in the soap factory where he would receive a steady income. But every time he thought about quitting he'd hear from Paul, a former cellmate who was moved into a hospital ward in a prison where there were no caregivers. Paul had yet to be stamped with an expiration date, and Hal had wanted to get him transferred here so he could look after him. That was during his first few years as a caregiver. By the time Hal no longer heard from Paul, he'd already decided to stay a caregiver.

He insists the decision is not selfless, that he enjoys his work. Helping guys (he calls them "guests") around with their wheelchairs, helping the ones too feeble to sit up, or with hands too shaky to hold a pen write their letters. Making his rounds, passing the time with these men in conversation or in comfortable silence, playing checkers, dominoes, and just simple things like fluffing their pillows and straightening their blankets for them, and giving them holiday and birthday cards, all of it, he says, is rewarding, and actually selfish on his part because it makes *him* feel good, makes him feel appreciated, and gives his life purpose.

With all due respect, I had to tell him that he could have it. He'd told me about having to get used to the stench of incontinence and the stinging bite of the ever present smell of urine, and how it's important to train your face not to show the slightest discomfort, and that deodorizers were out, that the guests should be allowed to pass their last days with dignity, not embarrassment. That's all good, but it just ain't me.

Still, it was an honor to know Hal and to be his friend. I'm going to miss him. He had a major stroke last week. After the guards rolled up his property, the chore of cleaning out his cell was left to me, since I work here in the building. The guards didn't pack his box of recycled cards, and the box of used cards that need to be trimmed with new cover paper. I figured I'd hang on to it, in case he ever came back. I'd be here, I'm an L-WOP too. But I found out this morning that Hal won't be coming back, he died yesterday.

Maybe some night I'll set up his card stand, try to keep it going. But not tonight. I'd found something else of Hal's that day. I kept it for him, and now I have to do something with it. In the bottom of one of Hal's boxes of cards I found a bunch of letters, one hundred and two, to be exact. All from Hal Anderson to Sarah Anderson, his daughter. None of the envelopes have postmarks, nor stamps. I checked for dates on the letters themselves, which spanned a decade. I read some of the letters, Hal expressing regret and remorse, laughter and loss, apologies and attempted reconciliation, and some were simply to let his daughter know that he loved her and was thinking of her.

Me, I'm just sitting here in my cell thinking about Hal. I wrote a letter. I don't know if I'll send it. I'm not sure if I should. I dunno ... Lemme read it again:

"Dear Sarah,

You don't know me, but I was a friend of your father, Hal Anderson. Your father was a true friend to me. He showed me how to make my way when I first came to prison. Your father helped me earn my GED. This pen I'm writing with, it was a graduation gift from your dad.

He always told me how much he regretted not being there for you. He said he tried many times to find you after your mom moved, not an easy thing to do from in here. He never told me, but I guess he eventually found you. I say this because recently a stack of letters somehow made its way into my hands. Letters from your dad to you. From the dates it looks like he started when you were in your late 20's. But he never mailed them. Maybe he was unsure of how you'd react after such a long time, and so he kept writing while working up the courage to send them. Unfortunately, now he won't get the chance. His spirit was paroled last night.

I know in my heart that your father wanted you to have these letters. He loved you very much. He once told me that a person's essence lives on in his writing. So I'm sending you these pages of his soul. Please read them and get to know him..."

NO BEAUTY
IN CELL BARS

Spoon Jackson

Restless, unable to sleep
Keys, bars, guns being racked
Year after year
Endless echoes
Of steel kissing steel

Noise
Constant yelling
Nothing said
Vegetating faces, lost faces
Dusted faces

A lifer
A dreamer
Tomorrow's a dream
Yesterday's a memory
Both a passing of a cloud

How I long
For the silence of a raindrop
Falling gently to earth
The magnificence of a rose

Blooming into its many hues
Of color
The brilliance of a rainbow
When it sweetly lights up the sky
After a pounding rainfall

Picnics in a rich green meadow
We saw the beauty in butterflies
We made it our symbol
Tiny grains of sand
One hour glass
A tear that may engender
A waterfall

The memories
The dreams
Are now
Love is now
There's no beauty in cell bars.

YOU'RE IN PRISON

John Purugganan

It's not like in the movies. That stuff really happens, but it doesn't all happen in an hour and a half, in three acts that build to a dramatic conclusion, like it does on the big screen. You think it's going to be exactly like that, especially after you've been convicted and sentenced, and you're still being housed at the county jail, and some guy asks if you've ever been to the "pen." When you tell him no, his face expresses grave sympathy and a grimace of pain. This is meant to communicate that unimaginable horrors await you. Movie scenes of brutal rape and blood-dripping shanks flash through your mind. All the other repeat offenders make a point to extend their heartfelt condolences about your impending arrival in certain hell. But you also overhear these same former convicts, these prison ambassadors of good will, talking among themselves about how they can't wait to get back to the pen. The contradiction first confuses you, then gives you hope. Maybe they just get off on putting a good scare into people. You tell yourself there's really nothing to worry about. Whatever happens, you'll deal with it. You have no other choice.

Then you talk to your brother Brian on the phone. "Are you OK?" he asks. "Are you nervous? Are you scared?" (He's seen those same movies.) You tell him you're OK. You're not nervous. You're not scared. Brian is silent for a moment before he says "What if someone tries to rape you?" You assure him someone - the rapist or you - will have to die. You'll fight to the death before you'll ever let something like that happen. Brian doesn't miss a beat: "But what if fifteen guys hold you down, and you can't fight?" You ask him is he trying to cheer you up, or is it just coming out that way? "Sorry," he says. "But you've seen what happens in the movies." Yes, you tell him, you've seen what happens in the movies. God! Let the nightmare begin already.

You arrive. Old Folsom State Prison. It looks old - spooky, too: forty-foot walls made of giant blocks of granite; black iron gates interlaced with barbed wire; towers capped with Gothic, conical roofs. Your first thought is of Count Dracula's castle. The place was erected in the days when prisoners were executed by hanging. They buried the bodies right there, on the infamous China Hill. You hear ghosts calling from the graves as your bus descends into the ancient compound.

But you soon discover the real nightmare is more mundane. Simple freedoms you once took for granted are stripped away, such as taking a shower when you need one (never mind *want* one). The real horror about prison showers is not the threat of some bald-headed, three-hundred-pound degenerate sneaking up behind you. No, the real horror is the sight of an empty shower, a shower that is within spitting distance of your cell, where you sit stinking and sweating and not knowing if anyone will be permitted to enter that shower today.

There are numerous similar predicaments in prison, but you won't see them in the movies; a producer would be shot in the head for producing such monotonous rot. The endless continuum of boredom is enough to make you lose your mind. You can't dwell on it, or you'll spiral somewhere you do not want to go. So you don't think about it; you don't talk about it; you'll write no more about it now.

Your sister Teresa asks how the guards are treating you. No complaints, you tell her. Don't mess with them, and they won't mess with you. Many of them have been here longer than the men they are guarding.

Sandy, your younger sister, asks about the other inmates. She wants to hear about the monsters. You tell her quite honestly that this is the most polite society you've ever known. In 1990 Old Folsom is still in the long, generally peaceful aftermath of the seventies riots, and for the most part, everyone seems content. If someone inadvertently bumps shoulders with you, it's not an occasion for posturing or picking a fight; he will look you in the eye and respectfully excuse himself, and etiquette dictates you should do likewise.

"Aren't there any tough guys in there?" she wants to know. They're all tough, you tell her. But they're smart also, smart enough not to incite unnecessary conflict.

"Oh," she says, almost disappointed. You realize that on some level, not so far beneath the surface, she *is* disappointed. She wants a traditional prison horror story. She doesn't understand that this is not a Hollywood movie; it's not even an independent film.

"Well," she goes on, "what about the guys who lift weights all day? Do *they* give you any trouble?" It's been your observation that the bigger the inmate, the more mellow he seems to be. Pumping iron all day works off his aggression, and he gets a good night's sleep. He's not interested in you or what you're doing, so long as you're not out of line. Big muscles command respect in prison. The bigger your muscles, the less likely it is you'll be required to use them.

Sandy asks if you work out. Only on the typewriter, you confess. You do play basketball, a little cardio to help prolong this charming life.

Your brother wants to know if there is a lot of homosexual activity. You're happy to report, there is very little - not that you have anything against homosexuals, but the old-timers have told you that, "back in the day, if you didn't get yourself a punk, then you were going to be one." It was "do unto others before they do you." Now, thanks perhaps to homophobia or fear of AIDS, the horrid practice of making someone a "punk" has been abandoned. That's not to say that two men cohabitating in a cell as man and punk is entirely unknown.

The "man" will claim *he* is not gay; his cellmate is. He's living in the closet with the door wide open.

This was not the type of movie your siblings were counting on. Had you known that they would one day abandon you to your fate, you might have juiced up the script to keep them in the theater. You'd like to think you have a little more integrity than that, but, at the moment, you feel so ... Well, let's just say you were unprepared for the avalanche of returned letters, for the automated voice on the phone informing you that the party did not accept your collect call. Again, you can't say you were surprised, exactly, but you didn't entirely see it coming. You can't help but think things might have been different if you'd livened up the narrative, given them the grim penitentiary tales they so desired. There are some: Child molesters invariably make horizontal exits strapped to gurneys, their destination either the county morgue or an intensive-care unit. Gamblers and junkies with outstanding debts are typically dealt the ignoble shank, precisely inserted into the neck. Loudmouthed drunks occasionally murder each other for no sober reason. These deaths are accompanied by little or no fanfare, but maybe you should have shared the stories anyhow, strictly for entertainment value. Your brother and sisters might still be talking and writing to you.

In your head you have the absurd image of Brian, Teresa, and Sandy assembling in a Howard Johnson's restaurant for an impromptu sibling meeting - with you absent, naturally. The meeting comes to order with no preliminaries. Sandy daintily dabs the corner of her mouth with a paper napkin and makes the motion: "Let's just drop his ass." The motion is seconded, with some reservation, by Brian. Teresa says, "Whatever," distancing herself from any potential guilt, should it arise. The meeting is adjourned. Let the record reflect that the sibling condemned to prison is hereby excommunicated.

Just like that? How dare they! What happened to the guilt complexes your beloved mother and the Church so diligently heaped upon all of you? There was guilt for every occasion - in your case enough to fill an entire book. It's not possible that your sibs emerged from the experience unscathed. At any rate, you object! You'd like a chance to defend yourself before you are convicted. You were under the impression that a newfound sense of family unity had been discovered during your arrest and trial. They even hung in there with you through the first few years of your incarceration. So why have they abandoned you now?

Fine. You never asked for them to be your siblings anyway. Bad luck and random genetics forced them upon you. Of course, you're kidding yourself; you'd welcome them back into your life with open arms. No words will ever adequately describe the long, dark nights in prison. Your sarcasm, your cinematic allegories, your weak attempts at wit, your bitching and moaning are all a front. You're projecting onto them your own guilt, your own sense of shame, which time will never erase.

Twenty-three years ago you moved from Hawaii to California with your wife and your six children. For the previous twelve years you had worked in the food-and-beverage industry, and now you'd decided to start your own catering company. But first you'd treat yourself to a little break from work. You'd held down two jobs most of your adult life; you owed it to yourself to relax a little.

That first hit of crack cocaine had you hooked: heavenly bliss. As your daily consumption increased, your savings account diminished. But you'd quit soon enough. Just one more hit, one more blast. Your "little break" from work lasted for more than three months. It ended with you strung out on crack cocaine, another man's blood on your hands. You'd never met him before that terrible night, the fourth straight sleepless night of a crack binge. You were looking to score another bag of rock. Paranoia soaring, you became convinced he was setting you up. You believed, wrongly, that it was kill or be killed. His name was Carl T.

Carl T. never saw his thirty-fifth year. He did not marry his lovely fiancée. He never fathered the children he'd hoped to have one day.

His dreams were never realized because you went over the edge. You took Carl T. with you. You did not bring him back.

You can say you're not the same person anymore; you're not that cocaine-addled, paranoid schizo who killed Carl T. But it doesn't change the fact that he is gone forever. And that his father's eyes still haunt you.

You remember your brother and sisters were offended by the way the T. Family was eyeballing you in court. "You should see how they're looking at you, man," Brian said. But you had seen. More than you could bear. One glimpse of Mr. T's eyes was all it took. You averted your gaze. You couldn't handle what you saw there. Beyond Mr. T's anger, beyond his hate, beyond all the reasonable responses to your crime, you saw the fathomless void of another man's sorrow. It was a taste of what you might feel if someone killed one of your children. Anger? Sure. Hate? Without question. But all the hate in the world could not begin to fill the void you saw in those eyes. The void you had put there.

You did not dare raise your eyes to Carl T.'s mother.

You were unable to articulate any of this to your family. You told them only that if they said one word to any member of the T. family, you would never speak to them again. Your brother was incredulous. "Why don't you fight?" You were fighting, of course, but not with the T.'s. Your fight was with the state, which had charged you with first-degree murder. You never denied killing Carl T., but it was not premeditated.

Over the years you've written several letters of apology to Mr. and Mrs. T., letters you could never bring yourself to send. You didn't seek their forgiveness; you know you don't deserve it, and it would be selfish to ask. If they did grant forgiveness, it would only serve to make you feel better, and at their expense: the final insult.

Of course there's more. There always is....

Every father in prison is guilty of a greater crime than the one he was convicted of. He has forsaken the most sacred of trusts: he is a deserter of children.

You were going to be the best father there ever was. You'd earn the right to wear one those silly T-shirts that boast, #1 **DAD**. You'd have worn it with pride. When you were a kid and home life was a perpetual celebration of dysfunction, you'd thought, *It doesn't have to be like this!* You'd vowed, in spite of anecdotal evidence that we are destined to repeat our parents' mistakes, that you would have a good relationship with your children. You'd never scream at them or talk down to them. You'd take time to explain things to them, even when you didn't feel like it. Never would you say, "Because I said so!" - that horrible euphemism for "I don't respect you enough to explain why." If one of your children brought an unfair situation to your attention, you'd take the necessary steps to correct it. Together you'd figure out what was fair, and it would become a rule. This would be your family policy.

By the time you had a three-year-old, a two-year-old, and a two-*month*-old, you considered that there might be more to it than that, and perhaps you should educate yourself on being a parent. You went to the public library and began checking out all the parenting how-to books. Some were filled with philosophical fluff, and most others had a central theme of controlling your children through manipulation or intimidation. Of course, they didn't call it that. They used tidy phrases like "reverse psychology," "strong encouragement," and the all-too-readily accepted "tough love."

Unrelenting, authoritarian drivel.

Ah, but you're getting carried away again, aren't you? You're blasting these authors and their well-intentioned efforts so that you can avoid looking at your own misdeeds as a parent.

You eventually found a gem of a book that said children are people just like adults, only smaller, and they're at our mercy, so we should treat them fairly. With help from this book, your children were developing into more than responsible individuals: they were reasonable, caring, and remarkably kind human beings. They weren't perfect, but they were a pleasure to be around. You once overheard one of your daughters telling her older sister about a girl at school who had hurt her feelings. "I thought she was my friend," your little girl tearfully confided, "Now I never want to see her again."

Big sister, all of seven years old at the time, responded, "Sometimes kids are mean because they don't have anyone to be nice to them at home. That's what Daddy says."

Memory is sweet, even as your heart breaks. You taught your kids that there are reasons people act the way they do - not excuses, but reasons that sometimes deserve our understanding. Besides, being bitter and judgmental is no fun. It could have been your subconscious, planting seeds of forgiveness that you hoped could later be harvested on your behalf. You never came close to being the BEST DAD EVER. Even before you completely deserted your children, you'd spent more time at work than at home. Your children's mothers (you've been married and divorced twice) are the ones who fostered gracious manners in your offspring. They are the ones who clocked the long hours of perseverance and patience.

Your children remain your greatest joy. You hope they are doing well. You were completely cut off from them a year after your arrest. You continued to write to them, not knowing if they ever saw a word, because there was still so much you wanted to share, to teach them. Instead of litanies of do's and don'ts, you wrote them stories and songs. You told them how much you loved and missed them. You asked their friends' names, and their teachers', and what they'd learned in school - anything to show them you were interested, that you cared. Your letters went unanswered. For eight years you clung to the hope that they were at least receiving the mail you sent. That hope dissolved when the last parcel was returned to you with no forwarding address.

You rarely talk about your kids. They own your heart and soul, yet you hardly ever mention them. You're a mess when it comes to your kids. Hell, children in general. You choke up at the sight of a jolly, diapered baby crawling across the kitchen linoleum in a

TV commercial. In the corniest of movies, the quivering chin of a child about to cry makes your eyes pool. Yeah, you're a mess.

When you visit your children in your dreams, they are the age they were when you last saw them. Each time you awake from such a dream, you want to go back to sleep, to return to that time in the past. There are moments when you'd like to go to sleep and never wake up. But you must go on. You must live with the pain you have caused others, knowing you can never make amends. You cannot give Carl T. back his life. You can never return Mr. and Mrs. T.'s son to them. You will never be able to make up for all the times your children needed you and you weren't there. And these only top the list of your many transgressions.

You will die alone in prison. Still, all is not lost, not yet. This is not a movie, but you can still hope for a relatively happy ending. If you can achieve even a small amount of success with your turns on the typewriter, maybe you can leave something for your children besides the memory of a crackhead father who abandoned them.

Hope, despair: these are facts of life. Sometimes they seem to go hand in hand, when you're in prison.

BEAUTY IN CELL BARS

We lock ourselves up
not because of the bars and
steel that surround us
not because life doesn't bend
to our every whim

But because of the projections
we place onto our worlds
The judgments, the I can'ts
The trying to please everyone
while not pleasing ourselves

By seeking the beauty on the outside
that is surely within
For prisons are created internally
and are found everywhere

We allow unnatural and unreal thoughts
to be our walls, our limits
Because of the dam we build to
stop the universal love, the light

It's all within ourselves
this paradise you go to of beauty
and love
There's peace, where along with the
eagle you may soar
A place inside that was inspired
from the inner and above
which are one and the same

The world may not bend to
your every whim
But it will flow wherever you
want it to go,
where it's supposed to go
There's beauty in cell bars.

LIFE WITHOUT

Martin Williams

Twenty-two years ago I was given a life-without-parole sentence. It seemed about right. A death sentence might have seemed worse; it's a strange alternative to a life in concrete boxes. Either one would have made sense.

Now I understand how choices multiply into other choices. One could choose death over a concrete box; if the box, one could choose to become narrow and cramped, or to go within, into the real prison, into the real demons and inner dopefiends and cops and thieves of his own heart, his own head. The stuff of prison's got nothing on the stuff of basic human-ness. Everything that imprisons I already am. Until I learned this little truth, I had no business judging the system that decided at some point that a life in concrete was merciful compared to death.

While in the box my mother died without me. While in the box lots of people died without me. Technology changed to the point that I doubt I can even make a phone call.

I got old.

Of course, that's the narrow story, the story that comes from being crammed in square holes. Yes, it is life-without-parole. But it's still life. Screw parole. In a world of staggering bad choices, between choosing life or death, the choice between embracing the without-paroleness of my existence, or the *life,* life was mine before I ever thought to choose it.

Stay now
now that the earth spins ashes at the stars...
It is morning and I creep awake
into an anxious silence
that was once for prayers.
The year is gone,
the good year
of a green and deathless spring,
a summer's toil. In Autumn
it rained, and just now
the morning sun attempts
to find me through dirty glass
and stretch along a gray
faceless wall. I would
send back the day
for a moment more
of the prayerless dark
if I could.

I lived crammed in holes for several years when I first came to prison; holes of prison rules, white rules, masculine rules, holes of fear, of religion, of identity-seeking and faith in the god of suicide that hovered brooding over the empty waste. I played cards, dominoes; watched *Cheers* and jacked-off frequently. I became a popular figure on the yard, a valued worker, a mainstay on the weight pile. I slept in the chemical wakefulness of meth, in fantasies of the past, in creative projects that were nothing but toys to keep my mind from slipping away. My greatest fear was not death, but going crazy, and I saw plenty examples of both. Yet another weird, staggering choice to make.

But stay now, now that the earth
spins ashes at the stars
and remember the poets
who sat among the potsherds
and broken totems of their tribes
wrapping grief in tongues,
who sat upon the hearths,
upon the severed marble heads,
songs resounding off silent tels
turning our lives to myth,
the scroll of Everyday unwinding
with each broken seal.
Stay now, maybe one last time,
like dry seeds
in expectant earth.

Then I began to choose things that were, in my belief, beyond, above, outside me. I read philosophy. I read Jung, Campbell, Hugo and Milton. I was more entertained by Shakespeare than the *X-Files*. I had a book called *Fourteen British and American Poets*, and I read them all many times over, and even believed that I understood Eliot. I wrote my own poetry, won awards. I slowly dissolved from the card games and hanging-outs and fierce demonstrations of my worth. The late night manic vibe of crank began to work against me; I no longer tried to escape, or fit in, to the without-paroleness of my sentence. Life called from the silent concrete pre-fab sealed by the immeasurable weight of a society helpless to deal with or confront its own shadow, which is we in the box. I wanted *life*, with or without anything, crazy life, unknowable life, gameless and placeless life.

Somewhere there are bricks
laid by immigrants
into the walls of alleys

where sometimes poets slept
between MadDog and matins,
saxophone prayers in halfsteps
caught in a century of mortar
while streets turned gray,
while Bird and Coltrane
turned to myth,
while blues went to Chicago,
while none stood at the crossroads
with a price on their soul,
no more seller's remorse
in all the bent a'dragging notes,
the earth a jazz of perfect fifths
that mask the flaws that make
beautiful our cry.

I would prefer no pain over certain pain. I'm not that crazy. And I would prefer a hand to mouth existence where I could walk in a forest of smells and unseen chitters than an existence of free toilet paper and a five-dollar dentist visit. I haven't been seduced by prison. It's a hideous bland face pressing into every area of your life, senseless with racism, adolescent violence, infant rage, administrative apathy, ignorance, insanity, despair, and multiples of worlds within worlds that seem interesting, but aren't. It combines into a vast, hideous bland face. And the main enemy to prison is life, growth, creation. Plants are illegal. Green is olive drab and belongs to the cops. Blood is to be spilled, staunched. Love is weak. Affection is gay. Life is an enemy.

I choose life. I choose the enemy. I am the enemy. I cry, like a baby I cry. I greet the grass with bare feet. I greet the moon with a full heart, every star that somehow appears through the false light of the prison's night sky. I teach others to teach themselves music, art, ways to pray, to hope, to be angry, to greet the grass with bare feet. I am alive. Life hurts and I welcome hurt; I choose the hurt. Life caresses and heals, and I choose it. I choose it like crazy.

Before an existence of staggering bad choices, between concrete and death, when I had the whole world to breathe in, I never greeted the moon. I never sat on a cold concrete floor in mindless prayer to a God who makes no prisons, who makes no prisoners, who is an alien to punishment and fear. I was without parole and life altogether.

I choose life.

I choose the enemy.

But stay now
and remember the scarecrows
heaped in Auschwitz trenches;
remember the gilded cry
of temple horns on the morn
before Christ died.
Remember the sprinkled laugh
of children before the infamy
of age, the eternity that lingers
before the touch of lovers' lips.
Remember most musicians
fade unheard, most poets
lie buried under piles
of dead trees,
that hope
is tenacious curiosity
in what the world will be tomorrow,
flaming blue ball of smokey glass
spinning ashes at the stars
maybe one last time.

So stay.

DEAD MAN LIVING

Spoon Jackson

I must keep pulling myself up the rock mountain, and my legs and arms and hope are all old now. I must keep creating hope out of nothing, each day, indeed each moment.

But sometimes it seems, after 10, 20, and 30 years in prison, the only hope, the only freedom I have left is death.

I came into prison barely a few days after I'd turned 20. I had never been inside a prison before. I have not seen any of my 20's, 30's, or 40's on the streets. If by punishment you wanted me to feel great pain, sorrow, empathy, suffering, guilt, worthlessness, and to feel inhuman, you accomplished that decades ago. So perhaps it is time to focus the light on yourselves. People do change and do better in prison, as surely as darkness can turn to light. As thinking, feeling, spiritual human beings, hope must be offered even to the worst of us.

There must be a way for society to forgive its criminals. Yes, I'll never be a saint, not even counting that egregious error I caused that brought me to prison. I'll continue to make mistakes, but I'll strive each moment to be a better me. Instead of walking into things blind, I'll fly into them with my awareness and eyes open. My actions show now I do better because I know better. The wayward, uncaring and unseeing, badass kid that I was has shed his skin and sprouted feathers and wings. He can soar.

A prison counselor told me there is no hope. "Mr. Jackson, you have life without parole no matter what you do. You are an LWOP and you'll die in prison no matter what. Life without parole in California means life without parole."

Will death be enough? I have died a thousand deaths. Death sometimes seems way more real and promising than living an LWOP sentence. It's like if I fart the whole world hears and smells it, yet still I am alive. I know - when considering the State of California's politics of racism, injustice, and inhumanity in order to keep their prisons packed - my hope to someday be released is like hoping to be one of the first people to live on Mars.

What is the use in carrying on if I never get to smell the sea, or sniff a flower, or sit in the shade of an apple tree? What is the purpose of pushing on if I never get to stroll in the forest, or walk up mountain trails or down desert paths? If I never again see the stars at night. What is the meaning of continuing to struggle if I never get to make love again, kiss and hug again? Never again to eat real vegetables, fruit, fish, or meat, or to live around the people I want to live around. Never again to be alone, to smile, cry, or sleep for hours.

Yet, I am a fool, because after 34 years - although I am broken-hearted - I still hope to climb that rock mountain. I hope to keep my spirit and heart alive and prospering.

I hope to hold hands again.

THE MEANING OF LIFE

Joseph Dole

Rarely am I ever asked what it's like to serve a sentence of life without the possibility of parole, and, understandably, it's not something often contemplated by the public. The State's Attorney on the other hand, when arguing for the death sentence for my first felony conviction, implored the judge not to allow me to spend the rest of my life on a virtual "vacation" in prison. Having never read an accurate conveyance of what life without the possibility of parole feels like, and while I lack the skill to adequately depict such a feeling, I can assure you that it is no "vacation."

Life without the possibility of parole can mean a million things, because, as its name implies, it encompasses the entire remainder of one's life. So what does such a sentence *really* mean?

It means that after being "spared" the death penalty and receiving life without the possibility of parole, you lack all the procedural safeguards against a wrongful conviction that a traditional death sentence would have entailed, solely because you were found undeserving of a quicker death.

It means that courts will turn a blind eye to any act against you unless it causes "atypical and significant hardship." A free man may find protection in the courts from emotional and mental harm, but a prisoner can only find protection from "atypical and significant" physical harm. So when you're stripped naked and left in a concrete box with nothing but a toilet for four days without cause, as a prisoner you have no recourse in the courts. Or when you're beaten to a bloody mess while handcuffed, as a prisoner you're more likely to encounter a jury that will automatically conclude you deserved what you got, no matter what the circumstances are.

It means enduring decades of discrimination from both the public and the courts, you're not even worthy of being considered a second-class citizen, you're lower. In this country a condemned man's entire character is defined by whatever derogatory remark the media or popular culture chooses.

It means a lifetime of censorship, where you're told what books and magazines you're permitted to read, what movies you're allowed to watch, even what hairstyles you can have, and where every letter coming in or going out is subject to inspection.

It means a complete lack of privacy forever, and a complete indifference to your physical and mental health until someone fears being sued.

It means a constant, heightened risk of catching a deadly disease. You're captive in an environment where drug resistant strains of staph infection run rampant, where people still die from tuberculosis, and where the population as a whole has twice the rate of HIV infection, and where up to forty percent are infected with hepatitis. It's an environment where there's nowhere to hide from these diseases, and you're forced to use communal toilets and showers.

It means three meals a day of the poorest quality food that the least amount of money can buy without killing the inmate population.

It's a daily existence where trust is non-existent and compassion is not allowed. Not only is compassion viewed as a sign of weakness in the prison milieu, but it is, ironically, actively discouraged by the prison administration. If your neighbor is destitute and you want to assist him by giving him soap, paper, or even a snack to supplement the meager meals, you can only do so at risk of being written a disciplinary ticket for "trading and trafficking."

It's a never-ending pressure cooker where the stress and anxiety compound daily as you have to watch your back at all times. Our military members returning from Iraq understand this. It's a major factor in Post-Traumatic Stress Disorder.

The constant fear for your safety and the need for 24-7 situational awareness frays your nerves. Now, imagine not a 12-month tour, but a lifetime deployment.

It means you're constantly being told that you aren't worth rehabilitation and thus are ineligible for nearly every educational or vocational program. Your life sentence disqualifies you from any state or federal grants to pursue an education. Even the Inmate Scholarship Fund (which was founded by a prisoner) has no qualms about telling (or should I say fortune-telling) you that you're ineligible for a scholarship because you're never going to get out and contribute to society.

It means convincing yourself daily that your life has value even when the rest of the world tells you you're worthless. It's a lifetime spent wondering what your true potential really is, and yearning for the chance to find out.

It means decades of living with double standards, where any guard having a bad day can call you every profanity ever invented without any fear of punishment, but where if you utter a similar response, or anything that even resembles insolence, you'll be written a disciplinary ticket, lose all privileges, and be subjected to a month of disciplinary segregation.

It means missing out on every important event in your children's lives, unable to raise them, impotent to protect them or assist them in any meaningful way. It means they'll grow up resenting you for the thousands of times they needed you and you weren't there.

Life without the possibility of parole means constant contemplation of a wasted life, and continual despair as to your inability to accomplish anything significant with your remaining years. A life spent watching as your family and friends slowly drift away from you, leaving you in a vacuum, devoid of any enduring relationships.

It's a persistent dashing of hopes as appeal after appeal is arbitrarily denied, as well as a permanent experiment in self-delusion as you strive to convince yourself that there is still hope.

It's a compounding of second upon second, minute upon minute, hour upon hour, of wasted existence, and decade upon decade of mental and emotional torture culminating in death. It's a death by incarceration.

But I digress; these are simply futile attempts to describe the indescribable. It's sort of like trying to describe a broken heart or like trying to communicate what it feels like to mourn the death of your soulmate. You can't find the words to convey the pain. When you're serving life without the possibility of parole, it's as if you're experiencing the broken heart of knowing you'll never love or be loved again in any normal sense of the word, while simultaneously mourning the death of the man you could have been and should have been. The difference is that you never recover, and can move on from neither the heartbreak nor the death because the pain is renewed each morning you wake up to realize that you're still here, sentenced to life without the possibility of parole.

It's a fresh day of utter despair, lived over and over for an entire lifetime.

WORSE THAN DEATH

Tracie Bernardi

The reason you put a fence around an area is because you want to make either entering or exiting difficult. The fence that surrounds me is the kind that keeps you in, locks you up and throws away the key. It's much more than a careless line drawn in the sand. It represents the division between general society and those of us who have gotten caught.

But is it the fence that keeps us separated or is it society's inability to accept that people who make mistakes are capable of change?

Many believe that the death penalty is the worst of the judicial system, but there is a fate worse than death. It's known as the other death penalty, life without the possibility of parole.

How can life be worse than death? Imagine living a life without a point, a reason, or a direction - breathing but never living.

I am incarcerated and serving a thirty-year sentence. It is my testimony that being sentenced to life without the possibility of parole is even more cruel and unusual than a traditional death penalty.

Many would argue that at least the convict sentenced to the other death penalty can still breathe fresh air; many victims don't even have that option. Perhaps that's the position lawmakers take in determining the penalty at sentencing.

I am not writing to defend anyone who has been convicted of a crime. I believe every society must maintain law. Those, like me, who commit crimes should be held accountable. I simply do not agree with the way America penalizes people in some cases. America favors punishment over rehabilitation.

Why do we waste billions of dollars every year building and maintaining prisons and calling them Correctional Facilities? Obviously the name speaks for itself: "Correctional," to rehabilitate, improve, or to be corrected. People in prison participate in rehabilitation so that *when* they are released they can enter back into society, emotionally healthy and whole. The word "when" entails a light at the end of the tunnel.

Some of us, however, do not get that chance. We participate in groups, we grow into healthier people capable of transitioning back into society. Yet, we're not afforded the chance because of our lengthy sentence. No matter what we do, how much we grow, it doesn't make a difference. We're still held captive behind the unforgiving fence.

There has to be a change in the law, in order to make a way for a second chance. I recognize that some convicts are irredeemable and should not be released at any time. These decisions should be determined by psychiatric specialists appointed by the court. Lawmakers try to push some career criminals out of the system in order to save taxpayers' money. They think handing out 90-day sentences will curb the recidivism rate. How could a person effectively utilize the rehabilitation opportunities within a correctional facility if they are released as soon as they arrive? It takes months for people to get on the waiting list for programs. Some people leave prison and mess up, which makes it difficult for lawmakers to trust that other people, given the opportunity, will not do the same thing. However, I believe decisions should be made on an individual basis, not by group broadbrushing.

Obviously, there are many different cases and scenarios that come into play when discussing release policies, yet, I believe sincere people should be rehabilitated and transitioned back into society.

I've been incarcerated since March 17, 1993, and I am leaving prison in 2017. Although it's still 5 years away, I *can* go home. I came to jail at an early age, and I look forward to learning how to drive, learning how to cook. If I make it home before I reach menopause I may even have the chance to bring a life into the world.

I will leave this prison breathing.

My best friend here has a different fate. She will leave in a body bag. No matter what she does, she will never see the other side of this fence.

That's too cruel, and, sadly, not unusual enough.

JUST A MATTER
OF TIME

Charlie Praphatananda

Why is life without the possibility of parole the death penalty? The answer seems obvious to me. I mean, "life without the possibility of parole" - that couldn't be more obvious, right? It's pretty much spelled out to the letter.

There are a lot of people sentenced to life without the possibility of parole and every situation is different. Yet every one of these experiences has certain defining universals. If you have this sentence, then you can understand its tombstone finality. There's no more doing what you want, no waking up in your *own* bed at home. There's no anything, just four walls staring back at you and a stranger sleeping either below you or above. Your existence is as a number, a bed space.

Many prisons allow the purchase of personal tv's and radios, other prisons only provide communal sets. Like the narrow window of a cell, broadcast programming offers a dreary view: daytime/nighttime soaps, reality retreads, vapid talk shows, sensational fluff that passes for news. Yeah, you kind of get an update on popular culture and current events, but it's cookie-cutter stuff; it's broadcast world, not real life.

For those of us in prison, the years grind down our senses and time ceases to move. I have a friend named Tino, a few years younger than me. When I was still out there, Tino's dad had a rule for everything, one being "No girls allowed in the house." After I came to prison, after a number of years had passed, I called him. To my surprise, a girl answered his phone. When I asked Tino who she was, he replied "my girlfriend." I laughed and told him he better not let his dad find out. This was met with silence, and then he asked me, "You know I am over 18 now, right?" Then it hit me – all along, *in my mind,* I had aged but Tino had not.

When you're incarcerated, you don't have recourse to intellectual programs that would allow your mind to grow, and you're certainly not allowed access to the internet. So when you're released, you lack the cognitive and perceptual skills to function in the real world, which is so much larger, so much more complex and bewildering than the tidy happenings you watched on television for decades. In time, you could adjust; your mind would be like an atrophied limb that slowly regains function after the cast is removed. However, there's no such recovery for those of us sentenced to life without the possibility of parole. The cast around *our* minds isn't a temporary one of gauze and plaster; it's a permanent, unbreakable one of concrete and steel.

Most prisoners arrive here with little or no education. And it usually stays that way. There's never been a consistent presence of educational/vocational programs in the prison system, just some remedial reading classes and sometimes a GED class. For all the folklore of the incarcerated getting Ph.D.'s en masse, the reality is, even a two-year Associate degree is beyond the financial reach of the few with a high school education. Since 1994, the federal Pell Grant has been off-limits to prisoners, and most states don't include the incarcerated as possible recipients in their scholarship programs. Still, most incarcerated people do eventually re-enter society and so at least get the *chance* for continued education. However, those of us with life without the possibility of parole don't, and that's the difference.

This isn't a debate about whether people sentenced to life without the possibility of parole *deserve* education or not - that's a different question altogether. I'm just pointing out that the incarcerated *don't* have any real access to education, and we life without the possibility of parole prisoners *absolutely* don't, because we're confined to the restrictions of prison forever.

In prison, why can't you just read books and periodicals to keep your mind alive? Prison libraries are *law* libraries, mandated by the courts to provide tomes of statutory codes and case law. Non-law books and periodicals are a fiscal afterthought, and consist mostly of cheap fantasy novels and fad magazines, with a local paper or two sprinkled in - meager fare for the mind. Yes, in prison you're allowed to purchase your own books and periodicals, but you're tightly restricted as to the type and quantity, subject to "penological inter-ests" and "institutional needs," which really just means the whimsy of whichever guard happens to be working that day. It's a moot point though, because in prison you simply don't have the money to make reading materials something you can regularly afford; whatever few dollars you get, you have to save up to buy toothpaste and soap, espe-cially with a 55% restitution fee out of all money received. Still, when you re-enter society, you can read all you want at your local library. But those of us sentenced to life without the possibility of parole can't, ever.

All of us know what that sentence means, or at least we think we do. We understand the language, the wording which clearly states that there will be <u>no</u> chance of a second chance. Of course, none of us *really* believes this.

The first peg of hope is always the appeal. For those who actu-ally are innocent, they start out staunchly confident that the truth shall prevail, only to realize after all the briefs, motions, and writs are done, how hollow is the promise of exoneration so casually trumpeted by death-penalty abolitionists who tout life without the possibility of parole as a morally acceptable alternative to the traditional death penalty. What they too casually overlook is that unlike the traditional death penalty, the other death penalty - life without the possibility of parole - doesn't come with *any* of the many legally mandated checks for making sure a person hasn't been mistakenly convicted.

As for those who are not factually innocent, we're still human beings and we still hope for some kind of sentence modification. When that doesn't happen (on average, 5 years in, after all appeals are exhausted) we must figure out what to do with our next 40 to 50 years of incarcerated existence. Many of us lose ourselves in drugs or prison mayhem. Others try to take the high road and stay busy with exercise or religion, but either way, we're slowly but surely dying. It's hard to stay positive without the basic qualities of what it means to be a whole human being. When you know it'll all end the same way no matter what you do, then your spirit dies, too.

Socially speaking, prison is a grab bag of misfits, small-time crooks, con artists, mental patients, deviants, sociopaths and predators, all governed over by watchful, angry guards. Better character doesn't develop from this melting pot of cast-offs, just the splicing of bad traits, the trading of tricks-of-the-trade, the molding of uber-rejects who encompass the worst of each type. For anyone to claim that we're socially alive in here because we interact with *each other* - well, that's just plain offensive, and ignorant at best. Being socially alive means interacting in a *healthy* way, not constantly trying to avoid being manipulated, oppressed, or attacked by the next guy. In the rare instances where we form genuine friendships in here, those friendships always hinge on there not being a riot, a transfer, or one of the myriad upheavals that regularly uproot prison populations and scatter friends to the four winds. In here, we're all acutely aware of this inherent instability; it deadens many of us so we don't even bother trying to humanize with others in prison. For us, the only prospect of any lasting social ties is with those on the other side of the razor-wired, electric fences.

However, most of us incarcerated people don't come from stable backgrounds to begin with. Any bonds we might have are weakened by time, age, distance, and the general limitations of prison.

Letter writing is supposed to help, but it rarely does. "Real heart" letter writing requires a willingness to honestly express true feelings and open up to emotional vulnerability, a chasm of risk that most of us in prison are unable to leap. In here, having feelings is regarded as weakness and the daily rigors of survival snuff out the basic sentiments that are the core of humanity. As for our loved ones out there, it's nothing so dramatic. It's mundane. The daily bustle of life is a constant river that washes away our family and friends' good intentions to write regularly. This is compounded by us not having anything new to say; for us it's usually the same old, same old.

Phone calls are available in limited time blocks (usually 15 minutes) and are expensive (long distance "collect call" rates only). They're infrequent. They're not a basis for sustaining relationships. They're more like a way to catch voice bits around the holidays, or to once in a while listen in on the sounds of real life.

As for visits, prisons are usually located out in the middle of nowhere, because bigger towns are unwilling to accept a prison in their backyard. For our visitors, driving long distances through winding remote roads is daunting, not to mention the high cost of gas, food and lodging, and then running the gauntlet of antagonistic guards in the typical prison's visiting area. Our visitors can be kicked out for standing up too long or holding hands with us too long. The reasons can be anything. If the guards take a disliking to us, our visitors are punished by being delayed in processing, or by being told to go back to change clothes. Most relationships end this way.

Then there's the horror stories of prison, the T.V. and movie portrayals of riots, stabbings, and a whole host of other atrocities and outrages that can't be soothed with words, that can't be eased with reassurances that this won't happen to you. These conditions dissuade most family members (let alone friends) from visiting on a regular basis. In fact, *only about 10% of all prisoners receive visits.* For those of us who do, the intervals between visits slowly get longer and longer apart. When we finally see our loved ones again, they seem more and more like strangers: more lines in the face, more gray hair, sometimes heavier, sometimes lighter, always a vague "differentness." The talk is awkward, stilted. Slowly, family and friends drift off, one by one. It's too much to deal with; they have lives to live out there. Most of us in prison understand. We're sad but still hopeful. We look forward to the day we re-enter society, when we can reconnect with our loved ones again. But for those of us sentenced to life without the possibility of parole, there's no looking forward, no hoping. Once *our* loved ones step out of the visiting room for the last time, we'll never see them again. Life without the possibility of parole also means *without the possibility of reunion.*

I've realized that life without the possibility of parole is the death of my heart, the death of me as a social person. I realized that it's too much to ask a girlfriend or wife to do time with me, because that's essentially what she's doing. I had a beautiful wife who showed me what it was to love and be loved. But coming from two different worlds, it became too painful for her to handle. The stress of us constantly going on lockdowns, the guards beating people up and getting beat up themselves, the hardships of coming up here to see me began to take their toll. The constant harassment by the visiting guards and the hour-and-a-half delays during visiting took their toll, too.

I felt it coming before it happened. One day she came to see me. In the moment, her presence put me at ease; my cares, troubles, and doubts about life all ceased. However, I felt it. I suppose she could see it on my face because she asked me, "Is something wrong?" I told her, "I can't help but feel this is the last time I'm going to see you." She smiled and told me it wasn't, but I knew it was. And it was. Being that I am a life without the possibility of parole person, I was helpless to do anything about it. I couldn't say it'll only be for a few more years, or anything else that could soothe the pain I'd caused her by being locked up with life without the possibility of parole. That was the first real relationship blow my heart ever took; it messed me up pretty good.

The next blow to my heart was with the birth of my niece. It was then that I realized I'd never have a family of my own, never have kids and all the other things I'd taken for granted. I'm not the first to come to this conclusion.

It's been fifteen years since I was sentenced to life without the possibility of parole. It's been a growing experience. The totality of what my sentence means has left me with an overwhelming sense of loss.

I used to think, 'What a mess I've made of my life.' Life without the possibility of parole has shown me that it's not just my life I've made a mess of, but also many others. I've had to stop and look. I can't get away from the reality that I've hurt so many people: those who suffered directly from my actions, and their families and friends. And my own loved ones, too. I suppose that's one of the hardest parts of all this. Because accepting responsibility for those I hurt means I have to accept that I also hurt those closest to me. That's not an easy truth to accept.

In the end, I'm not sure how useful these realizations are, too little, too late. I can't change my past decisions. All I can do each day is try to make better ones.

The rest is just a matter of time.

LIFE

Christian J. Weaver

A skull on a stick
Or a corpse in a cage
Or a chest of old sweaters and bones

A convict so old
He forgets why he's here
Though he claws at the riddle for days.

He raises his fork
With mechanical hands
And his mandibles grind like a horse

His eyes are as blue
As a sky full of clouds
And as moist as a watery grave.

His Nutraloaf falls
Through a hole in his mouth
And it splatters unseen down his shirt

I watch him for months
He's quiet as death
Till I gather the courage to ask...

He's sixty plus three
Preternaturally aged
And he once had a kid by a girl

Can't think of its name
Can't remember her name
Ain't for sure if it's actually his.

"This greasy old food's
Gonna kill me some day -
Gonna die in the next year or two..."

He states a mere fact
Without pathos or wit
And I see that he's perfectly sane.

But hey, at least the son of a bitch
Didn't get the death penalty like he
Deserved.

THE FIVE STAGES OF LIFE WITHOUT THE POSSIBILITY OF PAROLE

Kenneth E. Hartman

It took me 25 years to realize I'd been sentenced to death. Until that dismal moment of clarity, I labored under the delusion I merely had a longer life sentence, that if I did everything I was supposed to do, if I worked hard enough and became a better man, the state would relent and let me back out.

When I first came to prison an administrator told me that no one serves forever, "everyone gets out, eventually," is what he said, to be exact. He wasn't lying because it was a true statement back in those days. But in between that time and now, a lot changed. None for the better, either. The rise of an old-styled punitive mentality, cloaked in the language of the new confessional tone of public discourse, replaced the ideal of rehabilitation with that of punishment for the sake of inflicting pain. Working to correct negative behavior was deemed pointless, at best, and a direct affront to the damaged sensibilities of victims, at least. Nevertheless, my peers still don't realize they're walking dead men, and our friends and families are caught in a similar state of misapprehension.

What those of us serving life without the possibility of parole, or what can be described accurately as "the other death penalty," need to come to terms with is it's not just a term of art; it's an accurate, literal description of our sentence, a sentence that doesn't contain within it even the *possibility* of parole.

When this harsh truth I'd deliberately looked away from muscled its way into my consciousness, it took my breath away. I then experienced all of the expected stages of grieving as I mourned the loss of the ephemeral hope I'd carried around within me for a quarter of a century of horrifying prison life.

DENIAL

Since I'd already spent a couple of lifetimes in denial, this part of the process went the fastest. I still clung to the same handholds we all do, the readymade deceptions we prisoners use to prop us up from drowning. Figments of desperation like the laws from back then were different so the state is now practicing an *ex post facto* enhancement of our original penalty, though that argument has died an ignominious death in courts all over the country. We, as a group, have always been too reliant on courts coming to our rescue. For those of us with decades under our belts, it's particularly irrational. We live in a country that believes it's reasonable to sentence serial check-kiters and pathetic dopers to interminable life sentences. The courts aren't going to wake up one day and decide a bunch of old guys who killed somebody should now be released in the interests of justice long delayed.

I'm glad I never fell prey to the truly irrational forms of denial of so many of my peers, the fantastic tales that circulate around the yard like tidal surges inundating reason, overwhelming common sense. There's always somebody serving the other death penalty being awarded a parole date in some other, distant prison, always a law being (secretly, of course) discussed that would change life without the possibility of parole, and always a court decision (again, secretly) that just overturned the whole edifice of being sentenced to the grinding, dissipating form of execution. Somehow, those who take refuge in this fabricated information never seem to be dissuaded by the stark reality of still being inside a prison the next year. Some prisoners fall into this trap so thoroughly it becomes painful to watch, as they bounce from one ludicrous fantasy to the next, yet keep waking up in the joint along with the rest of us, year after year.

But I suppose I did fall prey to a particular species of denial during my quarter of a century of willful blindness. I came to believe, to the very core of my being, that good works could rebalance the scales and restore me to the status of a full human being. I became a whirlwind of activity and positive focus. I founded prisoner self-help groups dedicated to the sole purpose of making the world a better place. I put my life in jeopardy more than once to stand against the rampant negativity of the prison culture. I actually made a difference, a real difference, in this world if nowhere else.

It's not that I regret the good I've tried to do with my life. I don't, not at all. Somewhere down inside of myself, down below the surfaces of my mind in the liquid dark recesses of my sub-conscious, a belief in redemption and restoration germinated and grew silent roots. Once I came to the full realization of how far from truth this belief was, how far from my personal place in the reality of the wider world, a part of me died right there on the spot. The part of me that held to the belief in rebuilding myself to reclaim my freedom moved on from this plane of existence. This loss of faith remains an angry spur that rubs me raw.

Still, like every other prisoner sentenced to die in prison, my heart leaps a little when I hear the latest irrational rumor of reform long delayed. I have to fight against the urges to start planning for my return to the rest of the world.

ANGER

It's easy to get angry with all of this, far too easy. And the list of reasons is long. No other country on earth uses this sentence with such a cavalier attitude. There are only a handful of other countries that have the other death penalty as an option, and only a relative few people are sentenced to it in all the rest of the world, compared to the more than 40,000 in the ironically misnomered Land of the Free. With a criminal justice system firmly rammed over to the punitive, reactionary side of the scales, with the practice of incarceration mutated into a monstrous sort of business, this doesn't come as a shock.

To realize the self-proclaimed progressive folks at the big civil rights organizations and at most of the death penalty abolition groups lobby hard to bury as many people as they can behind bars that can never open again, *that* is shocking. It's a good cause for anger, too. I find my stomach churning every time I hear the names of certain famous actors. The thought that these are people and groups in the liberal vanguard of our society leaves me speechless and spluttering.

Harvard Law School did a comprehensive study about their misguided Faustian bargain. Over the past decades that our abolitionist brethren adopted the slow, out of sight death penalty, in trade for the slightly quicker form they have only succeeded in slowing down a small part of the machinery of death. The other gears in the apparatus have more than taken up the slack as life without the possibility of parole has become a much more widely used, tolerable sentence, more than making up for the decrease in traditional death sentences. The whole truth of it is our "friends" on the left have made the other death penalty the socially acceptable form of execution, one that's now applied to many more people than it would have been absent their help.

It's easy to get angry at the whole criminal justice system, at the whole of society. Serving this sentence often feels like being stuck on a warped exercise wheel, always running to try and prove, for the umpteenth time, that I'm better than the worst moments of my life, that I'm more than the wail of a faraway siren, more than the contents of a long forgotten case file on a dusty shelf in some deserted warehouse. The whole process of administering life without the possibility of parole sentences is rigged in fundamentally unfair ways, contrary to the defenders of the system's too loud protestations of even-handedness.

There is anger aplenty to be directed at the mass of men and women serving life without the possibility of parole, as well. A group of often talented, intelligent, and creative people more often walking around in a daze of delusional thinking, sleepwalking in abject surrender, lost to the world, dead before they've breathed their last.

But the real anger, the white hot stuff that melts good thinking, that's reserved for the idiot that put me in here in the first place – myself. For the vast majority of us that are guilty, it's hard not to fall into some serious self-loathing. In my own case, as the decades have dissolved behind me, it becomes more difficult to conjure in my mind's eye the scenes of what happened at the nexus of this experience, let alone be able to project myself back into the ill-fitting shoes of wasted, misspent youth. All I am certain of is I committed a terrible act that I, apparently, can never finish paying for, at least not in this lifetime.

BARGAINING

Prisoners bound up in this greased slipknot of a predicament are fond of seeking out ways to bargain with society, with the Fates, with God himself. In our bargaining with this grim reality we hope that if we wish hard enough we could push our desires back in time to reshape the laws in the book we were crushed by after it was thrown at us all those years ago.

Toward this end of making a deal with society we become model prisoners, involved in every good program, and more than willing to go many extra miles to demonstrate through our actions how much we've changed. It's reasonable to bargain because the goal of any rational prisoner should be release, to not be a prisoner. And there's no doubt we, like all human beings, do change. The trouble is we can fall into the trap of becoming so focused on not making any waves we fail to stand up for our own humanity. I suspect there comes a reckoning one day concerning how much of us is left if we ever do get back out after selling off great chunks of ourselves for the chance, after decades of bowing and scraping.

There is also the complicating issue of the segment of society, loudly represented by the angriest faction of the victims' rights movement, that holds to the idea that there can be no bargaining with prisoners sentenced to the other death penalty. To these people, life without the possibility of parole must be, and always must remain, an actual death sentence. We have to die in prison regardless if this happens 50 or a 100 years later. To them, anything less, any scrap of a chance held by a prisoner is considered unacceptable. It is, in their minds and hearts, a kind of betrayal; it's an insult to them if there is even a theoretical set of conditions that could result in the release of one of the condemned, that could result in my release.

Prisoners in this country are faced with a well-funded wall of opposition that won't consider sitting down to a conversation about this subject. It's tough to negotiate with people who refuse to acknowledge your humanity, who refuse to accept your right to exist beyond the confines of a prison cell.

Over the years of advocating for change to this sentencing scheme, I've had occasion to correspond with a couple of folks wedded to the idea of mass perpetual punishment as the only appropriate outcome to their private loss. In their fury, there is no place for any bargaining; they can conceive of no eventuality that includes release. It's tragic for all concerned. But their extreme position has been elevated to the only position worthy of consideration. The collection of special interests that profit from the expansion of prison systems has invested heavily in promoting the punishment-only approach and suppressing the contrary ideas of redemption and restoration.

It is no less tough to try and make a deal with a society so thoroughly wedded to the idea of perpetual punishment as a fit and proper response to an expansive set of crimes. The logic, such as it is, holds that until the victim has recovered or lost interest in further punishment it is right to continue imprisonment. There is no objective standard to measure the extent of grief or to quantify sufficient suffering. When the reality is presented that this is but a system for the institutionalization of revenge, pain trumps reason in a culture dedicated to the primacy of the gut over that of the intellect.

DEPRESSION

Speaking from my own perspective of time running away from me, of the ferocious vitality of my younger years replaced by the aches and pains and arrhythmic heartbeats of a middle-aged man, there is a sadness to all this that's hard to evade. There are days now, whole days, when the overriding question devolves to a simple existential complaint: Why do I continue pushing against the stone of time? And I'm remarkably fortunate, having been able to build many profound connections to the rest of the world and father a wonderful daughter on a long ago conjugal visit who is still close to me after all these years.

The day-to-day reality of most prisoners serving the other death penalty is a far bleaker picture. Few ever receive a visit, get a card at the holidays, or have anyone to call on the rare occasions it's possible to place a call. It's an experience of premature death, of being erased from the flow of life, of becoming little more than a number filling out a cell in a table on a glowing computer screen backlighting a concrete control room.

Through the years, I've been forced to watch the overwhelming nature of life without the possibility of parole steal away too many minds. I've seen too many souls ripped out of too many old men trapped in the bodies of their younger selves' misdeeds. (As one close friend observed, "I'm being held hostage by my teenaged, idiotic self.") Not a one of them wouldn't go back in time to undo what sunk them into this concrete of unalterable consequence; not a one wouldn't change their path in life. Not a one isn't both ashamed and filled with remorse in equally choking amounts.

The heart of the other death penalty is the immutable nature of the punishment. Like all forms of execution, there is no possibility for change and growth. We are sentenced to punishment until we die for what we did in one moment of time, a moment that inexorably disappears from our consciousness like a bad dream fades away in the light of day. At some point, we all must come to terms with this truth. The end of the sentence, the end of the penalty, the end of the daily torment, is the end of our life.

Depression is a powerful force, one that has a comprehensive treatment plan in the psychologists' manuals and its own dreary language. For a variety of reasons, mostly revolving around the vaguely Teutonic concept of authentic experience, I've resisted the practice of medicating away the pain and suffering of being sentenced to die in prison. This is my life, in all its often-unbearable heaviness; I'm determined to live it to the best of my ability. I demand of myself that I feel all of this in its naked intensity, that I experience the full measure of the loss of my life, that I never allow the edges of the concrete around me to be rounded off and smoothed out too much.

But there are terrifying times when I feel as if I'm dematerializing, that I'm losing my purchase on reality, my hold on the rationale for continuing to walk to the chow hall. It's a psychic form of vertigo where the gravitas of existence all of a sudden relinquishes its grip on my being, and I'm floating above my life, drifting away. Thus far, I have always returned to my place in the flow of events and circumstances. Each time though the sadness of truncated desires and thwarted hopes is harder to shake. Each time, the thought of letting go becomes less unimaginable and gains a more solid foothold inside my unhappiness.

ACCEPTANCE

It is a kind of acceptance I practice, albeit one with a few caveats. I cannot accept that a practice condemned by virtually all the rest of humankind as a cruel and atavistic savagery should be allowed to continue unchallenged. I cannot accept that there are people who want me to shut up and die quietly so they can bargain away my life in a shortsighted deal with the executioners. I cannot accept that there is no possibility I can make a useful, important contribution to society from right here inside the joint.

I accept that I will die in prison. I now know that I was sentenced to death more than three decades ago for killing a man in a drunken, drugged-up fistfight in a little neighborhood park. I accept that what I did was truly wrong, and that I deserved punishment for my actions. I accept that society has a right to protect itself from angry, irrational young men acting out their internal misery on those unfortunate enough to get crossed-up in their turbulent paths.

Between the time when I draw my last breath inside a cell somewhere and now, I'll continue to do everything I can to urge my peers to wake up and reclaim their lives. I'll continue to speak truth to power demanding that we who have been sentenced to die in prison be afforded the basic human dignity of our experience being recognized for what it is, with an honest label, at least. I'll continue to call our hypocritical liberal "allies" out for their morally wrong decision to sell us out to salve their consciences.

With ever more focused energy, I'll keep standing on one side of the prison yard yelling at the top of my lungs that it's time for all of us to stop living on fantasies and falsehoods. Even though this doesn't make me the most popular guy in the place, I feel compelled to try and shake my peers out of their dejected torpor.

We who are serving this sentence, no less than the rest of American society, have been tricked by the mass media, by pandering, self-serving politicians and the prison-industrial complex into believing that life without the possibility of parole is a rational sentence. It is not. It is the definition of cruel and inhumane. In every other country, developed or not, rich or poor, it is also a very unusual sentence. It's high time this country's grotesque criminal injustice system is held up to more effective scrutiny. It's past time for the so-called progressive left to start speaking up for what they claim to believe in and stop bargaining away our lives.

Worst of all, we've been tricked by this culture into believing that it's just to be tortured for the rest of our lives inside prisons designed to be vessels of revenge. It's not just, and it's not a reasonable expectation. Life without the possibility of parole is, in actuality, life without the possibility of redemption. Not the state, not the parole board, and certainly not the victims get to make that determination. This peculiarly American concept of just deserts being the absence of forgiveness, the piling on of punishment for the express purpose of causing suffering, is wrong, period.

I refuse to surrender to the lie that a judge can strip me of my humanity. I will continue to work hard to reclaim my essential value through my actions. I will conduct myself with dignity even when it's not shown to me. I will live a compassionate and moral life regardless of where that life must take place.

TRUTH

I know, nonetheless, that death will find me here in the joint. I know I will never again breathe the air of a free man, no matter the duration or intensity of my struggle. My friends and family, no matter how much they love and care for me, cannot serve this sentence for me. They cannot lessen the horror of my life, such as it is. And I know, no matter how much I struggle to explain it, no matter how many thousands of words I scrawl, no one who hasn't been sentenced to die in prison can truly understand this experience.

LIFE WITHOUT THE POSSIBILITY OF PAROLE

THE VIEW FROM DEATH ROW

Joan Leslie Taylor

I am a visitor both of men on death row and men with life without the possibility of parole, so I welcome this opportunity to add my voice.

Back in a high school debate I argued with great fervor that the death penalty was morally wrong and unnecessary. My teacher gave me an A, but he said I was naïve and that when I was older I'd understand why the death penalty was needed. I'm plenty old now, and I still passionately believe that the death penalty is wrong and now I know more of why it's wrong, and why it needs to be overturned, not just for those on death row, but for everyone in any prison and for the health and well-being of our society.

Like many anti-death penalty adherents I once thought that life without the possibility of parole was a good alternative to the death penalty. At least people would be kept alive, so that if someone were found innocent, he could be freed. But life without the possibility of parole does not allow for the possibility that someone will be found innocent. Further legal proceedings are rare because life without the possibility of parole is a final answer by the system and innocence is difficult to prove from inside a prison cell. Life without the possibility of parole is the end of the road. All too many of those working to end the death penalty share the misconceptions and faulty reasoning I once used. They are in support of an abstract idea, not the people who suffer the ideas of others. They argue that if the death penalty is eliminated there must be a guarantee that the convicted person will never ever walk freely in our midst. Guarantee? There is not much in life that can be guaranteed, but one thing is certain: if you lock up a sizable number of young men for life, someday you are going to have a whole lot of middle-aged and older men who are no longer a threat to anyone, and it's going to cost a fortune to continue incarceration until death. And we will have cheated ourselves out of the potential contributions of all those who could well have been released after a fair sentence.

Until I came to know men on death row, it never occurred to me that being kept alive is not enough, and it's not solely because some are innocent. What kind of life are we so graciously allowing those saved from the death penalty?

After almost seven years of visiting men on death row who have become very dear friends, I can say without question that the people on death row are not all "monsters," or "the worst of the worst." They are surprisingly ordinary people, and as varied in experiences, abilities, attitudes, and values as any group in any place. A substantial percentage of death row residents have or had mental and emotional problems. Some had horrific childhoods without the love and caring of consistent parents. Some used drugs. Some fell into gangs. Most were young when they arrived on the row, and given time and the ordinary process of maturation, many grow out of whatever their problems were that led to violence. A small percentage should probably never be released from prison because they are too damaged to function safely outside a highly structured environment, and we don't have the knowledge or techniques to cure them.

But how do we know which inmates should never be released? The current law which dictates a life without the possibility of parole sentence at trial (or after a death sentence is overturned) assumes that the crime itself determines that no hope of rehabilitation is possible. And yet we know that some people go on from horrific crimes to become admirable and compassionate people with much to offer family, friends, and society. Purely from a logical perspective, wouldn't it make more sense to decide how long to keep someone in prison after having a chance to see how someone does over time? Life without the possibility of parole is a determination made at sentencing before anyone knows whether and how that person will change in prison.

Men on death row live every day with the knowledge that one day the state may execute them, but they all know that the process is long and slow and that many things can happen along the way. Not everyone on death row will be executed. As time goes on more and more of those condemned to death do die, but of the diseases of old age. A death sentence hanging over your head combined with a stressful crowded place to live takes years off your life. And yet there is also hope. Everyone on the row has appeals in process, and as long as an attorney is filing briefs and there's another court date ahead, there is always a possibility that the death sentence may be overturned, a new trial may be granted, there will be no execution, and some might even go free. Everyone I know on the row has hopes of one day walking free. It has happened for a few, which keeps those hopes alive for everyone.

Many on death row insist that if offered a choice between execution and life without the possibility of parole, they would choose death, but when it comes down to it, we are all human beings who are biologically programmed to fight for life. Almost no one "chooses" life without the possibility of parole, but there are moments in the appeals process that may lead to life without the possibility of parole. It is the most common alternative to execution, and looking at the big picture, it is the most likely outcome for the majority on death row. The appeals attorneys for those on death row see their job as fighting to overturn the death sentence, so getting life without the possibility of parole for the client is a win. Few attorneys hope to overturn the guilt finding, even when there is evidence that the inmate is probably not guilty. To overturn the death sentence is "good enough," and it is all that they are paid to do.

When I hear people calling for the end of the death penalty in California, I think of the 714 people sitting on death row, among them some of my dearest friends, and my heart is torn. I would be relieved to know that none of them would ever be murdered by the state, but I am horrified by the thought of sending 714 more people into life without the possibility of parole. I know one man who did walk off death row and into life without the possibility of parole, the forgotten cul-de-sac off death row. This man got his Associate in Arts degree while on death row, but where are the educational opportunities for him now? He has much to offer, and yet he has few opportunities to do more than survive another day, another year of incarceration. Life without the possibility of parole is indeed another death sentence. Human beings are treated like merchandise in a warehouse, and there are profits to be made for those in the business of prisons.

A life without the possibility of parole sentence assumes that the person is an extreme danger so he must be kept under the highest security, which precludes many educational and rehabilitative programs and also prevents those with life without the possibility of parole from holding the kinds of jobs that lead to new skills and responsibilities. The state feels justified in providing few programs for those who will never walk out of the gate. There are no plans for how people sentenced to life without the possibility of parole can live productive lives in prison during the long years ahead. Why waste programs on people who won't rejoin society? Life without the possibility of parole is a statement that we as a society have written off some of our citizens and we are only warehousing them until they die.

I have been privileged to know men in prison who have made inspiring journeys of personal growth and change, and I have read many prison memoirs, so it's clear to me that at least some people in prison, like some people outside of prison, do in fact grow and change beyond the dreadful mistakes and foolish acts of youth to become productive, caring, and compassionate human beings who have much to offer. Just imagine how many more people in prison might make that journey of change if prisons were set up to encourage and guide growth and development, and provided resources instead of obstacles and deprivation.

I am shocked that so many people, even progressive left-leaning people, buy the myth that once someone commits a violent act, forever after they are *ipso facto* a violent person, and violent felons should not be allowed out of prison. To be a human being is to have the capacity for awful violence as well as astonishing goodness, along with the ability to grow and change. I know that I have become a better person as I have grown older, so naturally I assume that others, including people in prisons, have this same capacity to evolve. In school I learned that in this country anyone, no matter how poor and deprived, can work hard and achieve their dreams. Life without the possibility of parole says the opposite and seems downright undemocratic. How can there be any justification in a democracy for writing off the lives of thousands of people in a scheme called life without the possibility of parole?

Although I came to death row believing that the death penalty was the problem, I quickly saw that it was only the most obvious part of a far greater problem. Prisons do not work, and the criminal justice system needs a complete overhaul. The theory of life without the possibility of parole is that if we lock up all the criminals, there will be no more crime and society will be safe. We must look at the sad results of the current system before any more laws mandating harsh new sentences are made. Instead of rushing to create a new category to be punished with a new and longer sentence every time there is a new awful crime, let's think about what we are trying to achieve. What are the causes of violence and how can it be prevented before the crimes are committed? And when someone commits a crime, what experiences and help does a person need to learn how to lead a productive and satisfying life without engaging in illegal and violent acts? We must move out of a fear and punishment based system that does not work, toward an evidence-based justice system with policies that reduce crime and provide prison programs that truly rehabilitate people who have committed crimes.

Too many people are making too much money under the current system, so it will take a major reform movement to bring about real change. As the death penalty exists, it will be used as a tool to force those accused of crimes to accept life without the possibility of parole, and as long as life without the possibility of parole exists, it too, will be a tool to exact lesser but still extreme sentences, all of which will fall most heavily on the poor and minority communities.

Ironically, the end of the death penalty and life without the possibility of parole may come, not because we realize it is wrong to execute a human being or to keep him locked away from the world until he dies, or because we have come up with a better idea, but because the state has run out of money and can no longer afford to lock up people forever. It's estimated that the death penalty will cost California a billion dollars over the next five years, and it will cost at least $875,000,000 over the next five years to incarcerate the 3500 people in California sentenced to life without the possibility of parole, so that's pretty close to another billion. While we pay the bill to incarcerate men and women who have long since aged out of the prime crime-prone years, a thousand homicides go unsolved every year in California due to lack of personnel to investigate and prosecute crimes. In this time when our schools are run on shoe strings, roads are full of potholes, libraries have shortened hours, services for the disabled are being cut, and millions lack basic medical care, we cannot afford the indulgence of the death penalty and life without the possibility of parole.

Although the idealist in me, who as a school girl argued against the death penalty, would like to think that California's citizens would rise up and say this must stop because it is wrong to treat our fellow human beings this way, if it is budget shortfalls that get people to reconsider the death penalty and life without the possibility of parole, let's take advantage of this opportunity to start the change that is so desperately needed.

WONDER AND SADNESS

Judith Tannenbaum

I taught poetry at San Quentin in the 1980's, back when California's oldest prison was also its most maximum security. There were 12 prisons in the state then, and fewer than 30,000 people inside (compared with today's 33 prisons holding more than 150,000 men and women). Almost all my students were serving some kind of life sentence: term-to-life, 99 years, life without the possibility of parole. Most had come to prison at or around age 20 and had been in close to a decade when we first met. Nearly all of these men are still inside, and the half-dozen I still write to are about to turn 53 or 54. All these numbers add up to the obvious facts that I taught at San Quentin a long time ago and that my former students have spent their entire adult lives in prison.

Spoon Jackson, one of these men, discovered himself as a writer in our class. Over the decades, he's published widely. A few years ago he suggested we write a two-person memoir and we did.

At one of the bookstore readings I gave for *By Heart: Poetry, Prison, and Two Lives* a man in the audience asked about hope. How, this man wondered, did Spoon - 33 years in on a life without the possibility sentence - handle hope? The questioner said that, of course, Spoon, like every human being, needed to hope to survive. But, if he hoped too much and too unrealistically, how could he stay sane and not become broken-hearted? In that audience were 3 of Spoon's

14 brothers and 10 of my many cousins; the conversation was energetic, personal, and painful.

How Spoon handles hope is, of course, his business. But if we citizens are going to put people behind bars for "life without the possibility of parole," I think we're obligated at least to wonder about what hope means in that context.

After my work at San Quentin, I taught poetry at a continuation high school. I walked into class one day having attended a Pete Seeger concert the evening before. I told the teen-agers what Seeger had meant to me when I was their age. I talked about the 1960's; how music was central to the Civil Rights Movement; how singing gave courage to young people (barely older than I was at the time I was describing and my students were that morning when we talked) as they faced police clubs, water hoses, and prison cells. I talked energetically about hope.

My students listened; they didn't even roll their eyes. But one in the circle said quietly, "I don't believe in hope." I was surprised and asked the boy to say more.

I don't remember his exact words, but in essence, he said that hope implied one knew the best thing to hope for. Hope seemed arrogant to him. Instead, he told us, he tried to have faith. I asked for his definition and he described faith as an awareness that what happened was what needed to happen.

Every high school student in that circle spoke in turn, and most agreed that hope was a flimsier substance than faith (trust, acceptance, reality; they used different words for what they tried to describe). These kids dealt with difficulty daily. Most adults in their lives wanted them to make changes, to do things differently, to have goals and dreams they worked toward. I supposed I wanted that, too, but I wanted more to listen to what the young people themselves found most useful and true.

I want to listen to my former San Quentin students, too. These men (who've now served many decades in prison) talk not only about the straight-forward hope that they will get out some day, but also about a more complicated desire for change in the forces against them (politics, racism, the voting public's hard heart). I hear my former students wonder how they can grow spiritually - which they say involves settling with What Is - while still being accurate about, and angry at, all they see stacked against them. How to accept, but not on one's knees?

Of course these are questions that arise in everyone's life. Even those of us whose lives are lucky know the AA prayer, which in Reinhold Niebuhr's original words asked for "...the serenity of mind to accept that which cannot be changed; courage to change that which can be changed, and wisdom to know the one from the other..."

I don't know the answer to the question asked in that bookstore reading. I don't know how Spoon - or anyone serving life without the possibility of parole - navigates hope. Spoon writes in *By Heart* that he'll never be happy in prison. He also writes about the sun on his face, watching birds, feeding cats, and reading letters from loved ones.

Of course, 54 year old Spoon is not the young man he was when he came to prison all those years ago; the man doing this sentence now is not the man who did the crime. In what world does it make sense to lock up someone just out of his teens for the rest of his life?

The other day, a friend - also a child of the '60's - told me that she couldn't do all the good work she does without believing that the world really will get better. I myself don't particularly believe the world will get better. I certainly *hope* that it will, but as my high school students pointed out in our conversation more than 15 years ago, hope feels pretty flimsy.

I do whatever I do - sharing poetry with children and people in prison, for one thing - not because I'm confident that these activities will make the world better in the future, but because the actions seem good in themselves right now. It's good to sit in a room with others talking together as openly as possible about beautiful, painful, real matters; good to write poems; good to have a space inside institutions (schools, prisons) where such humane things can happen. I hope, yes. But, as Spoon writes about his own path in life, my hope is "a melancholic mixture of wonder and sadness."

THE OTHER
DEATH PENALTY

Kenneth E. Hartman

More than 32 years ago, I killed Thomas Allan Fellowes in a drunken, drugged-up fistfight. I was sentenced to death. Not the more controversial death penalty, the one with high-powered lawyers and celebrities willing to stand in the fog outside San Quentin Prison in all-night vigils of protest. No, I was sentenced to the quieter and "less troublesome" death penalty, the one too many of those well-meaning activists bandy about as the sensible alternative to state-sanctioned execution: life without the possibility of parole.

Though I will never be strapped down onto a gurney and have life-stopping drugs pumped into my veins, be assured that I began the slow process of my execution some time ago—an execution in the form of a long and deliberate stoning that goes on for as long as I draw breath. My connections to the free world will be shattered as the daily humiliations of prison life beat me down. The endless rounds of riots, stabbings and lockdowns, the punitive searches and petty losses that characterize the life of a prisoner will, ultimately, batter me to death. Because I entered the prison system a couple of months after my 19th birthday, the stoning won't come to full effect for 50, maybe 60 years. I have often wondered if that 15 or 20 minutes of terror believed by so many to be "cruel and unusual" would not be a better option.

There is more to it than the mere physical act of imprisonment, much more. The 4,511[1] life without parole prisoners in California enter an unforgiving and bleak existence. We are condemned to serve out our lives in the worst maximum-security prisons, which are specifically designed to be punitive. This means that rehabilitative and restorative-type programs, the kinds of programs that can bring healing and meaning to a prisoner's life, are generally not available to us. The thinking goes that since we will never get out of prison there is little point in expending scarce resources on dead men walking.

Similarly, the prison reform community, with a few shining exceptions, cannot seem to run far enough away from us. On the one hand, there are the dedicated anti-death penalty advocates—who all too often advocate for this excruciating and grinding death penalty, and unwittingly legitimize the sentence—and on the other hand, those who are mostly concerned with re-entry programs. Needless to say, we do not fit into either category. Contrary to myth and legend, no one serving a sentence of life without parole in California has *ever* been released.[2]

What this means is dissipation—a gradual disappearance into the ever-expanding concrete and razor-wire empire of California's prison system. Family and friends run out of patience, out of hope, and out of our lives. It is understandable, though no less painful to experience. Imagine a close relative diagnosed with a terminal illness forced to stay at the hospital. Now imagine they hang on for years. They grow old and removed, and maybe a little bitter. Plus, this hospital is surrounded by lethal, electrified fences, and the windows are barred so tightly the light has to sneak in lest it be smothered by the shadows.

---

1 California Department of Corrections and Rehabilitation (CDCR) (2012) "Prison Census Data as of June 30, 2012" — August 2012, retrieved from www.cdcr.ca.gov.

2 Sundby, Scott E. (2005) *A Life and Death Decision: A Jury Weighs the Death Penalty,* New York: Palgrave MacMillan

At some point even the most kind-hearted, the most dedicated family members and friends will desire to be pardoned, paroled from being forced to touch this darkness.

I am a lot older now, and I am far removed from the reality of the free world. Truthfully, though I accept full responsibility for my predicament, and feel a crushing sense of remorse and guilt, I can barely remember the details of that terrible night all those years ago. Years that have moved on, stained by tears dried up in the hot wasteland of a life misspent. My own family abandoned me early on, perhaps sensing the torment that lay ahead. Both of my parents have passed and with them my hope for reconciliation. I have watched the world change so radically as to be unrecognizable. I have also watched, and suffered, as the prison system turned the screws on life without parole prisoners, gradually and inexorably squeezing us into a corner—not simply denying us release, but annihilating possibility itself.

Natan Sharansky,[3] himself a former prisoner, once observed that as hard as it is for man to come to terms with meaninglessness and infinity, it is impossible to adjust to infinite meaninglessness. I can think of no better way to describe the intent of a life without parole sentence. It is an exile from meaning and purpose, and from hope. Inevitably, as the years roll by, bitterness begins to overtake even the strongest of men, fueled by this banishing from all that is human. I fight the bitterness with all my might, faith, and love. But without hope, even these mighty forces seem inadequate to the task.

I agree that state-sanctioned execution is morally repugnant. I do not agree that a life devoid of any possibility of restoration is a reasonable or humane alternative. It simply is not. A death penalty by any other name is as cruel, as violent, and as wrong. While some prisoners may not be able to earn their way back into the graces of

---

3 Sharansky, Natan (1988) *Fear No Evil*, New York: Public Affairs

society, none should be wholly denied the chance. At the very core of our culture resides the concept of restoration, like a harbor light to the lost—extinguishing this light for anyone darkens everyone's journey. It diminishes all of us and blesses the basest of human instincts.

All forms of the death penalty need to be discarded in a truly just society.

THE PROBLEM
OF REMORSE

The Editors

How does one who committed the ultimate bad act, the taking of a life, address the subject of remorse?

In the writing contained within this short anthology readers will find multiple approaches to this brutally complex issue. A few go at it head-on, more allude to it through inference and analogy, and some elect to avoid remorse altogether. No doubt, if past is prelude, this omission will be seized upon by some as a great affront to crime victims and survivors. In an effort to explain this from the perspective of the prisoner, we offer the following rumination.

We've spent our entire adult lives in prison, and the number of guys in whom we did not perceive an overwhelming sense of shame for what they did that put them in prison is remarkably few. How this is manifested is complicated, nonetheless. At the beginning of a prison sentence there is a kind of psychic shock response. It's hard to feel anything. You're so overwhelmed with the horrific turn in your life it's all but impossible to feel anything beyond depression and denial.

Now, factor in the adversarial nature of our judicial system, as the new prisoner is admonished by appeal attorneys to never admit to anything, not in any setting. It becomes almost second nature to deny.

Family and friends don't want to hear the details of the worst moment of your life. They rarely ask for a description, one way or the other. Over time the practice of putting it all away in a box out of sight becomes ingrained.

Inside prison, generally speaking, there's a basic code of silence in regard to the nature of one's crime. Prisoners are not in the habit of sitting around and sharing their truest and deepest feelings. This world is not conducive to that sort of discussion.

Of course, there are innocents in prison; reputable authorities estimate the number to be as high as ten percent of the prison population. But the works in this compilation don't directly address innocence, and we elected to exclude that issue on the grounds that this isn't the right forum. The purpose of this is to allow decision-makers and people of influence the opportunity to see into the lives of men and women sentenced to life without the possibility of parole, the other death penalty; those condemned to die a long, slow death in prison.

Contrary to the popular rhetoric, "They're just sorry they got caught," many prisoners do feel great remorse for their crimes. Unfortunately, there is no viable forum for this to be expressed. Just as prisoners who experience religious conversions inside are ridiculed, and those who become educated are belittled, the few who have attempted to publicly express their remorse have been subjected to withering attacks, at least one of us included.

Ken Hartman feels tremendous shame and guilt for killing Thomas Allen Fellowes in a drunken, drugged-up fistfight more than 30 years ago. What he did was his fault, and he has formally accepted complete responsibility for his actions. For many, many years he's done all that he could to remake himself from what he was into a better man. Of course, he fully understands that nothing he ever does will undo what he did that terrible night all those years ago.

And that's the meat of the problem for almost all of us serving the other death penalty. We killed someone. Killing can't be undone. No amount of tears, no amount of furious efforts to become a better person, will result in death's reversal. And this is why we can assure you that not only does remorse exist behind these walls, it is a very big part of who we are in here. Because, almost inevitably, men and women in here eventually find themselves trying to do just that, trying to do the impossible, trying to undo the terrible acts they committed and trying to redeem ourselves. We see it all the time, in more men than you might imagine, men serving life without the possibility of parole. They might not be able to express their remorse with words, but they do express it, every day, with their actions as they strive to become better people.

For those who read this and question the issue of remorse we ask that you imagine how hard that really is to write about for anyone. Believe us, though, it's there, and it's felt everyday like an old wound that never heals.

CONTRIBUTORS

Too Cruel, Not Unusual Enough

CHARLIE PRAPHATANANDA

Charlie Praphatananda is a Thai-American serving a sentence of life without the possibility of parole. He has been incarcerated for the past 15 years. In 2008 he earned an Associate of Arts degree from Coastline Community College. In 2009 he co-founded the inmate activity group A.C.E. (Achieving College Education) which supports indigent inmates enrolled in the Coastline program. In 2009, he started volunteering his time to tutor inmates studying for their G.E.D. In 2012, Charlie co-founded the inmate activity group H.E.A.R.T. (Helping Everyone Attain Real Transformation). H.E.A.R.T. is the flagship activity group of the Progressive Programming Facility - aka the Honor Program - at California State Prison-Los Angeles County (CSP-LAC). H.E.A.R.T. facilitates the Lionheart Foundation's "Houses of Healing" class. In 2012, under the aegis of H.E.A.R.T., CSP-LAC was officially authorized as the first California State Prison to provide accredited DSST credit-by-exams from Prometric, Inc. In 2012 Charlie founded F.O.L.C.C. (For Our Local Community Charities) which donates crocheted items. Charlie currently serves as the Secretary of H.E.A.R.T. and Coordinator of F.O.L.C.C. In his spare time, he enjoys hobbycrafting, reading books, and meeting new people. He can be contacted at:

Charlie PRAPHATANANDA #T-05163
CSP-LAC A3-208
P.O. Box 4430
Lancaster, CA 93539-4430

CHRISTIAN J. WEAVER

C hristian J. Weaver is 34 years old. He is serving a life sentence in Tennessee for First Degree Murder; with a 51-year mandatory minimum sentence attached, life *with* parole is little consolation. He won't be eligible for parole until 2055.

A schizophrenic and an addict before committing his crime, while in jail he had a spiritual epiphany and his life ever since has been growth, renewal, and perpetual creativity.

Christian has been published in small magazines, including "Struggle," a socialist/unionist publication, and he won second place in the poetry category of the 2011 PEN fellowship contest for prison writers. His newspaper column in *The Pen and the Sword* had a 6-year run. He has written a collection of poetry, a book of essays and aphorisms, and a full-length play. He is currently writing a memoir.

DORTELL WILLIAMS

Dortell Williams is an incarcerated freelance writer. He has been published in a number of community and national newspapers and is author of <u>Looking in on Lockdown: A Private Diary for the Public</u> (Infinity Publishing, Conshohocken, PA 2010). He teaches creative writing as a peer instructor at the California State Prison in Los Angeles County and can be reached indirectly at <u>dortellwilliams@yahoo.com</u>.

JOAN LESLIE TAYLOR

In 1999 an attempt was made on Joan Leslie Taylor's life. Thrust into the court system she saw firsthand how "criminal" the system is and how little "justice" there is. She wanted to feel safe and to see that her attacker got the help he so badly needed. To her dismay, the system offered only punishment, and cared nothing for her or her attacker.

She came out of this experience determined to get involved. She attended execution vigils at San Quentin, and as she looked at the lights in the prison, she wondered who these men on death row were. In 2003 she began visiting a man on death row, and has since made many friends there, and is on the Inmate Family Council. In 2011, she married the man she began visiting in 2003. Despite the difficulties of prison and the looming threat of execution, they are very happily married.

Her published works include the book <u>In the Light of Dying, the Journals of a Hospice Volunteer</u>, and essays in <u>Tiny Lights</u>. She is the mother of two grown children and has five grandchildren. A retired accountant and tax preparer, she lives with her dog in the woods of Sonoma County.

JOHN PURUGGANAN

John Purugganan has been incarcerated since 1989. He wishes to thank Ken Hartman for inviting him to work on this project, and to commend all of the contributors, the writers, for sharing their talent, their words, their humanity. He can be reached indirectly at jcscreenplays@yahoo.com.

JOSEPH A. BADAGLIACCA

Joseph A. Badagliacca was born December 20, 1976 and raised on Long Island, New York. Currently, he is 35 years old, serving LWOP in Florida after being convicted at age 20 for Murder/Home Invasion Robbery. He has no other significant criminal history.

He dropped out of school in the tenth grade and has learned that you are always judged by who you surround yourself with.

Self-educated, he earned a G.E.D., Volunteer Literacy Certificate, and Law Clerk Certification while in prison. He became fluent in Spanish, taught English as a Second Language (ESL), and presently teaches beginner's Spanish. Due to his sentence and custody level no further education will be offered to him.

His mother remains his sole supporter. As a law clerk he continues his efforts to garner promotion of progressive change to LWOP sentences as well as the parole system in Florida.

He quotes Martin Luther King, Jr., "The time is always right to do what is right."

JOSEPH RODNEY DOLE II

Joseph Dole is currently serving a life without parole sentence for a conviction which he continues to fight pro se. He recently won a transfer out of Tamms Supermax in Illinois where he was isolated for an entire decade. His first essay was included in the book "Lockdown Prison Heart" (iUniverse, Inc., 2004). Since then he has written a number of articles, essays, research papers and proposals, two of which were catalysts for Illinois legislation (a bill and a resolution). He has won three PEN America Awards for his non-fiction essays, and is currently working on a book-length essay. He has been published in *Stateville Speaks Newsletter, Prison Legal News, The Journal of Prisoners on Prisons* (Vol. 20, No. 2, 2011), *Graterfriends Newsletter, The Insider Magazine*, and the *Public I Newspaper*, as well as numerous places online. Some of his work can be found on <u>www. realcostofprisons.org/writing</u>.

JUDITH TANNENBAUM

J udith Tannenbaum has taught poetry in a wide variety of settings from primary school classrooms to maximum security prisons. Her most recent books are "Carve This Body into Your Home: Poems and Collages," and a two-person memoir, "By Heart: Poetry, Prison, and Two Lives" (co-written with Spoon Jackson). Her other books include: "Disguised as a Poem: My Years Teaching Poetry at San Quentin," (a finalist in the Creative Non-fiction category of PEN Center USA's 2001 Literary Awards), two texts for teachers, and six other poetry collections. She currently serves as training coordinator for WritersCorps in San Francisco. You can read more about prison arts and teaching arts on her website, www.judithtannenbaum.com.

KENNETH E. HARTMAN

Kenneth E. Hartman has served more than 32 continuous years in the California prison system. He is the award-winning author of "Mother California: A Story of Redemption Behind Bars" (Atlas & Co. 2009), and has been published widely in newspapers and magazines around the country. Ken is the founder and Executive Director of The Other Death Penalty Project, a grassroots-organizing campaign to end all forms of the death penalty, including life without the possibility of parole. (www.theotherdeathpenalty.org.) He is also a co-founder and member of the Board of Trustees of Lifers' Education Fund, a scholarship granting nonprofit. (www.liferseducationfund.org.) And he is a charter member of the National Advisory Board of Californians United for a Responsible Budget, an organization dedicated to shrinking the size and extent of the prison-industrial complex. (www.curbprisonspending.org.) Ken is at work on a new book of lessons learned from a lifetime fighting for positive change, both within himself and inside the prisons. For more information: www.kennethehartman.com. He can be contacted indirectly at: kennethehartman@hotmail.com.

LUIS J. RODRIGUEZ

Luis J. Rodriguez has spent thirty years doing workshops, talks, readings, and reportage in prisons and juvenile lockups throughout California, other states in the country, and in places like Mexico, El Salvador, Guatemala, Argentina, and England. He is author of the best-selling 1993 memoir "Always Running, La Vida Loca, Gang Days in L.A." and is recognized as a leading gang intervention expert and urban peace advocate. He is co-founder of Tia Chucha's Centro Cultural and Bookstore in the Northeast San Fernando Valley, among other non-profits related to youth development and the arts. His latest book is another memoir, released in 2011 by Touchstone Books/Simon & Schuster, entitled "It Calls You Back: An Odyssey Through Love, Addiction, Revolutions, and Healing."

MARTIN WILLIAMS

Martin Williams has been serving a life-without-parole sentence in California State Prison, Sacramento for the past 22 years. He accepts full responsibility for his crime and has no beef with the consequences. He feels he still has much to be grateful for, and says the quality of his life is amazing. This is not to say he doesn't hate prison sometimes. Some days he hates it like death.

He never met his father; his family moved around like gypsies in search of work and avoiding bill collectors. His formal education did not exceed high school, although he once lived with a girl at SFSU.

He currently teaches music and art, and facilitates an Intensive Journal program, of which only 122 people in the country are certified for, with him being the only prisoner. He's been published and has won a couple of ribbons. He likes peanut butter without jelly and long walks on the beach.

His main focus is to continue to find meaning in the sterile gray box of prison, and to live at peace with the reality of himself, aware that he will often disappoint the people in his life who expect him to be something else. He simply refuses to wait for some condition to be met before he can begin being human. Being human is all he has left. And this is what he's most grateful for.

MATTHEW HUTCHINSON

Matthew Hutchinson is serving a sentence of life without the possibility of parole. He has been in prison since he was 18. Rather than becoming one of the walking dead that the state expects, he decided to use his incarceration to turn himself into the most positive example of why LWOP is not the correct way to go about doing things. He wants to show the world that change is not only possible, it is inevitable. He believes that everyone changes in prison and that we should be working toward making that change a positive one.

While incarcerated, he has learned to speak two other languages, earned a paralegal degree, learned how to draw, paint, and crochet. He uses his hobby craft knowledge to do charity work (making blankets, sweaters, and teddy bears for homeless kids). He takes college courses, and has spent an extraordinary amount of time fighting his case. Within the next year, he plans to have his book published. He wants to learn how to play the guitar, and hopes to start a business with his little brother.

He has received no assistance from the state's coffers; none is offered to those serving LWOP. He couldn't have achieved what he has without the help of his family. He feels very fortunate to have them, as the majority of inmates have no support whatsoever.

MICHAEL L. OWENS

Michael L. Owens is a 39-year old poet, essayist, and human rights activist. He has spent 20 years in the adult penal system, the last 14 in maximum security. His writings have been featured in the Haight-Ashbury Literary Journal and several other publications. He is the 2010 PEN American Dawson prize-winner for poetry. His debut collection titled "Foreign Currency" is available at The Freedom Now Society online or by mail at: M. Owens, P.O. Box 3441, Yuba City, CA 95992. He is a member of the advisory council for The Freedom Now Society, an organization focused on using art as a tool for social change. He is interested in possible collaborations and invites all correspondence to the address above or directly to him at:

M. Owens
J-25599
Box 290066
Represa, CA 95671

PATRICIA PREWITT

Patty Prewitt grew up on a ranch east of Kansas City. Her odyssey as a crime victim and then a hapless LWOP began in February of 1984. But from behind bars, this former cowgirl has earned her AA degree and received AFAA certifications as a group exercise instructor and personal trainer. Since 1995, Patty earns a living as a computer programmer and also designing eLearning modules. She's implemented an "inside" 4H club to strengthen family ties and hone parenting skills, reports for the prison newsletter, serves on the advisory board of Missouri CURE, designs and crochets teddy bears for charity, is an integral member of Prison Performing Arts, and won a PEN writing award for nonfiction in 2006. Currently on her behalf, Georgetown Law's Community Justice Project is seeking executive clemency (patriciaprewitt.com) and the Midwest Innocence Project is delving into her wrongful conviction. Patty is blessedly close to her four adult children, 10 grandchildren, and loyal flock of family and friends who suffer to bring her home to Lee's Summit, Missouri.

PATRICK ANGEL ACUÑA

Patrick Angel Acuña's mantra: Life without parole isn't life without hope.

At nineteen, an angry, insecure adolescent Patrick entered California's Folsom prison. He has since strived to become a man of decency and integrity.

Strong in his traditional Apache belief, Patrick is asserting his Jewish roots, studying Hebrew, while progressing in personal rehabilitation from a criminal lifestyle.

While incarcerated, for acting as a lookout in a robbery drastically turned murderous, Patrick has successfully earned an Associate Degree with honors in Behavioral Science. He co-founded Changing Within - an at-risk youth intervention program at California's SATF Prison; and served as an executive to the Men's Advisory Council, Native American Spiritual Circle, and Criminals and Gangmembers Anonymous (CGA) Ethics Committee.

Patrick is now incarcerated at R.J. Donovan Correctional Facility, where he is a Maintenance Mechanic with the Prison Industry Authority Laundry. In his spare time, he tutors inmates for the GED, functions as Chairperson of CGA-Donovan chapter, and pursues a Bachelor's of Mathematics with Ohio University. Currently, creative writing, in collaboration between San Diego State University and CGA, dominates his time. Patrick continues to write, recover, and make amends while living a life of hope and love.

ROBERT CHAN

Robert Chan is serving a sentence of life without the possibility of parole. In 2008 he earned an Associate of Arts degree from Coastline Community College. In 2009 he co-founded the inmate activity group "A.C.E." (Achieving College Education) which supports indigent inmates enrolled in the Coastline program. In 2009, he co-founded the Lifer's Education Fund (L.E.F.) a 501(c)(3) non-profit organization that provides scholarships for lifer inmate students who have demonstrated the ability to progress beyond the community college level. In 2012, Robert also co-founded the inmate activity group H.E.A.R.T. (Helping Everyone Attain Real Transformation). H.E.A.R.T. is the flagship activity group of the Progressive Programming Facility - aka the Honor Program - at California State Prison-Los Angeles County (CSP-LAC). H.E.A.R.T. facilitates the Lionheart Foundation's "Houses of Healing" class. H.E.A.R.T. also crochets clothing for local charities. In 2012, under the aegis of H.E.A.R.T., CSP-LAC was officially authorized as the first California State Prison to provide accredited DSST credit-by-exams from Prometric, Inc. Robert currently serves as the Chairman of H.E.A.R.T, and is a member of The Other Death Penalty Project, a grassroots-organizing campaign to end all forms of the death penalty, including life without the possibility of parole. In his spare time, Robert enjoys playing guitar, watching comedies, and reading all kinds of books.

He can be contacted at: Robert CHAN #J-30838
                           CSP-LAC A3-208
                           P.O. Box 4430
                           Lancaster, CA 93539-4430

ROBIN LEDBETTER

Robin Ledbetter is currently housed at York Correctional Institution for Women in Niantic, Connecticut.

"I am 30 years old now and each year I celebrate in here I can't believe how much wiser I am. I want to show people that change is truly possible. I am an example of that. All of these lengthy sentences for juvenile offenders are not justice."

Robin is still seeking relief for her sentence. She is very hopeful with the turn in interest regarding juvenile sentencing practices across the U.S. Robin spends her time working in the prison's medical ward as a nursing assistant, and in the prison's library, mentoring and studying. Her hobbies are writing, drawing, and performing her poetry.

"I love music, and I'm a huge movie fan. I also enjoy reading other prisoners' writings. The one thing that people are surprised by when they meet me is how normal I am. Prison has not hollowed me out. I'm bursting with life; I'm looking for the chance to live it, free!"

SPOON JACKSON

Spoon Jackson has been in prison for almost 35 years. He is an internationally known poet, writer, actor, native flute player, teaching artist and correspondent for the *Advocate* and for *Alt/Space* teaching artist journal. His poems are collected in *Longer Ago*, at lulu.com and have been featured in films, plays, articles, books and two music suites *Freedom For the Prisoners* and *Words of Realness*. He has won four PEN awards. He is featured in two films by Michael Wenzer: *Three poems by Spoon Jackson*, which won awards in five countries, and *At Night I Fly*, which won the Swedish Oscars for best documentary 2012. His newest book, "By Heart," was co-authored with Judith Tannenbaum. Contact Spoon at www.realnessnetwork.blogspot.com, and at

Spoon Jackson, B-92377
CSP-LAC/A2-231
PO Box 4430
Lancaster, CA 93539-4430

TRACIE BERNARDI

Tracie Bernardi, 38, has spent half of her life incarcerated at York Correctional Institution. As a teen, she sought acceptance in a gang, which lead her to the crime for which she is still imprisoned. During her two decades behind bars, Tracie has taken advantage of every opportunity afforded to her. She loves to write and is a member of Wally Lamb's writing group. She has also accumulated 24 college credits. Unfortunately, due to a lack of financial resources, Tracie may have to wait to be released to obtain her bachelor's degree. But, when she sets her mind to a goal, she follows through, despite the obstacles. Upon her release, she also plans to work in prison advocacy, as well as with "at risk youth" toward gang prevention. Tracie also plans to open a therapy oriented arts/ craft shop.

Tracie Bernardi welcomes input/feedback: Tracie Bernardi #2221434
201 W. Main St.
Niantic, CT 06357

EXHORTATION

The Other Death Penalty Project

NOW WHAT?

From The Other Death Penalty Project

What can be done about the other death penalty? Here are some suggestions.

1. Sit down and write a letter to one of the big death penalty abolition groups and ask them to stop supporting life without the possibility of parole as an "alternative" to executions.
2. Write a letter to the governor of your state and ask him or her to commute all death sentences, including life without the possibility of parole, to life *with* the possibility of parole.
3. Write letters to your elected representatives (state and federal) and ask them to introduce legislation that would ban all forms of the death penalty, including life without the possibility of parole.
4. Ask your religious leaders to speak out against all forms of the death penalty, including life without the possibility of parole.
5. Join The Other Death Penalty Project at www.theotherdeath penalty.org.

Life without the possibility of parole is a death sentence. This is a simple truth that cannot be denied. It is a morally inconsistent position to be "against" the death penalty yet "for" life without the possibility of parole.

It is time for the whole truth of the other death penalty to be told and confronted. The Faustian bargain struck by the death penalty abolitionist movement has resulted in more people sentenced to die in prison, not less. Just as bad, their acceptance of forever sentences has legitimized this practice, providing the ballast for the ever-expanding prison-industrial complex.

The only way to change the reality of more than 40,000 prisoners sentenced to die slowly in prison is to mobilize all of our resources, all of our talents, and all of our connections to others and speak out in a loud and clear voice: *Stop sentencing people to death by imprisonment.*

Made in the USA
Lexington, KY
21 February 2017